"If you're searching for peace, calm, and relief from anxiety, *Finding Rest* will help you find those, not just because of what the book focuses on but because of *who* it focuses on. True rest will never be found outside of the One who created it, and that person is Jesus Christ. Jon's found that to be true. I've found that to be true. And I believe, through reading this book, you will too."

KIRK CAMERON, actor and producer of *Revive Us*

"In *Finding Rest*, Jon Seidl offers significant help to those suffering from mental health issues and those caring for loved ones who do. Having known Jon as both his pastor and friend, I know this book has been birthed out of a deep conviction to address a topic that sadly has often been shunned in Christian circles. I admire his courage and believe this is a great resource for the church. Jon draws on Scripture and his own experiences to help people unashamedly plot a healthy course through the murky waters of mental health issues. Honest, practical, realistic, and full of hope, this book points us to Jesus, the One who gives us rest for our souls."

AFSHIN ZIAFAT, lead pastor of Providence Church, and council member for The Gospel Coalition

"All Christians need to understand a truly biblical perspective about mental health issues like anxiety, OCD, and depression. Jon shares that brilliantly and carefully here, supported by stories of his own challenges, decisions, and great victories. Your view of God, His love for you, and your trials will change in all the best ways when you read this. You may feel known for the first time. If you're the friend of someone who struggles, you'll understand them and their doubts more than ever before. Everyone will find compassion, great hope, practical power, and spiritual inspiration in these pages. You won't be overwhelmed or shamed. In a perfect world, everyone would read this book."

DR. KATHY KOCH, founder of Celebrate Kids, Inc., and author of *Five to Thrive*

"For those anxiety, thi tual journe gle and find

the why of their iences and spiritual race your strug-

sional counselor

"There's often an unfortunate hesitancy among Christians to admit that we too battle anxiety and depression. The quest for perfection and the confusion that can envelop us is often overwhelming, even suffocating. But in *Finding Rest*, Jon Seidl offers a raw and selfless look at his own struggles and victories, sending us on a thought-provoking journey toward our ultimate hope: Jesus. Seidl masterfully breaks down the pathway to peace that is desperately sought by so many."

BILLY HALLOWELL, author and journalist

"This book is unflinchingly honest, gripping, and full of truth that points readers to our Creator and the purpose for which He put us on Earth. It's for everyone: most, if not all of us, know someone or love someone who battles anxiety or OCD. This book gave me a deeper understanding of these mental struggles and greater empathy, enriching how I interact with those who are fighting internal battles I may never see. Jon also has a talent for dropping nuggets of gospel-centric truth that will resonate with me for years. This is essential reading for both the individual believer and the community of believers."

DAVID UBBEN, sportswriter with *The Athletic*

"Jon's voice is a powerful and necessary force in today's world. With a graceful balance between practicality and spirituality, Jon shares his story of walking through the dark woods of mental illness yet claiming victory along the way. His honesty blazes the path as he leads us bravely into the most vulnerable parts of anxiety and how we talk about it. This is a manual for anyone who needs to know they're not alone and that God is in the fight, carrying them through the fire."

HANNAH BRENCHER, author of *Fighting Forward* and *Come Matter Here*

"Now more than ever, so many people are fighting mental health battles and desperately need hope. They need to know they're not alone, they need someone to tell them it will be OK, and they need a guide that shows them why. Jon Seidl is that person, and *Finding Rest* is that guide. If you are tired, beaten down, and looking for hope, these words will be water to your soul."

MEGAN ALEXANDER, *Inside Edition* correspondent, and author of
Faith in the Spotlight

"Everyone needs this book—executives, students, parents, pastors, leaders. Even if you don't struggle with anxiety yourself, this book will help you support those in your life who do. Jon leads an open, honest, and thoughtful exploration of what it means to experience depression and anxiety as a Christian. He gives room for questions, yet provides clear answers that many are searching for."

BRIAN AND GABRIELLE BOSCHÉ, authors of *The Purpose Factor*

"I was with Jon the day he first told the world his secret about battling anxiety. I've seen the change in his life as he's implemented the principles he talks about, and I know that God is working through them. *Finding Rest* is powerful: anyone with a mental health struggle needs to read it and find the rest that Jon has found in Jesus."

JOHN HUMPHREY, executive producer for I Am Second

"If you or someone you love is dealing with the torture of anxiety, Jon's relentless vulnerability about his own hardships will bring you the words of peace you've been desperate to hear. Jon has not only struggled but is still struggling, and he lays bare his heart and his failings as well as his continuing progress to healthier living and understanding. In Jon, you'll find a kind, empathetic, and humble friend. In the God he leans on, you'll find true rest and help."

ADAM GRIFFIN, coauthor of *Family Discipleship*

"God has used and redeemed Jon's struggle so profoundly and powerfully that he has learned to see how God works all things 'for your good and His glory.' What an extraordinary message! Every page of *Finding Rest* is packed with tangible and timely wisdom. Anyone who is fighting a mental health battle needs to read this right now."

RAJ NAIR, media director for the Israel Collective

"Mental illness is a topic the church often avoids, which is why this book is so important. Through his own story of anxiety and OCD, Jon shows us how to be honest and vulnerable about our struggles—and how to have hope and joy even in the darkest moments."

DAVID ROARK, executive producer of the *Culture Matters* podcast, and coauthor of *Take Heart*

"Oh my. This book. From the very first paragraph, I knew I'd found a safe place among its pages. Jon Seidl's raw and compassionate exploration of anxiety, depression, and OCD in the life of today's Christian gives a voice to those of us who wonder if we're irreparably flawed or faithless. (Spoiler alert: we're not.) *Finding Rest* will rip away the stigma and shame that a misguided church has saddled on believers who struggle with mental health issues. Best of all, it guides us toward practical coping skills that strengthen our faith without suggesting we simply need more of it."

BECKY KOPITZKE, author of *The Cranky Mom Fix*

"As a pastor entrusted with many stories filled with mental health struggles (including my wife's battle with OCD), I can't tell you enough how much this book is needed right now. The way Jon humbly weaves the weaknesses of his own story with the truth of the gospel is so honest, refreshing, and powerful. If you're looking for hope in the midst of the hard, then you need to read *Finding Rest*."

JOHN ELMORE, senior director of pastoral care at Watermark Community Church, and author of *Freedom Starts Today*

"As someone who has been through the valley of depression and written on the topic, I love what Jon Seidl has done in *Finding Rest*. His stories are incredible, his steps practical, and his takeaways powerful. If you're looking to take control of what's going on inside of you, then you need to read this book!"

BEN COURSON, best-selling author of *Optimisfits* and *Flirting with Darkness*

"In nearly a decade of cultivating leaders, especially within churches, I've consistently seen that when mental health, and specifically anxiety, is discussed, the results are often disappointing. That's why *Finding Rest* is so important. Not only does it give those who are suffering practical tools, but it also gives church leaders the steps they need to take to better support their staff and congregation. I have learned so much from Jon in these pages, and I know you will too."

HOLLY TATE, senior vice president of growth at Leadr

"If you want to be a better manager, boss, or leader, then you need to read this book. Even if you don't struggle with anxiety yourself, you need to understand what those around you and under you are going through. *Finding Rest* gives you the tools to do just that. Read it for yourself, then give a copy to every manager in your organization."

KEVIN PAUL SCOTT, CEO of ADDO Worldwide, and author of *The Lens*

"From the personal stories, to the humor, to the nuggets of truth sprinkled like bread crumbs throughout, *Finding Rest* is powerful. Jon shows how faith and practical advice can coexist for anyone struggling with anxiety or other mental health issues. And the beauty is that he doesn't speak just to the sufferer but to those around them as well. Everyone needs to read *Finding Rest*."

JASON ROMANO, author of *The Uniform of Leadership*, and host of the *Sports Spectrum Podcast*

"As a survivor of mental illness, whenever I see a person of God share their story, I celebrate that we are one step closer to breaking down the stigma and releasing God's shameless love. Jon Seidl shares his incredible story with great courage, vulnerability, and wisdom, confronting the complexities and unpredictable nature of anxiety and OCD and finding rest throughout it all. With his refreshing insight that mental health is a balance of mental, spiritual, and physical well-being, you will be comforted that you are not lost or alone, that Jesus is not mad at you, and that there is hope for a full and meaningful future."

SARAH E. BALL, author of *Fearless in 21 Days*

"Even the strongest, most influential leaders can and do have mental health struggles. Those struggles do not care who you are or what you do for a living, and they can strike fast. If it hasn't already happened to you, then you need to be prepared in case it does. *Finding Rest* shows you how to fight back. Jon's clear and concise writing is something that leaders need in their toolbox, if not for themselves, then for those around them who may need it as well."

STEVE FRENCH, founder and president of L^x Partners

"More people are struggling with anxiety than ever before, but you can find steps to peace and victory through the experiences Jon Seidl shares in *Finding Rest*. An incredible writer and person, Jon combines humor, storytelling, and truth in a way that disarms. You won't want to put this book down."

MATT BROWN, author of *Truth Plus Love*, and founder of Think Eternity

"With so many people struggling with anxiety today, I'm so glad Jon took the courageous step to tell his story, ask the big questions, and share what has helped him along the way. This is not a quick-fix book—and that is a good thing. You will find helpful wisdom here, either for yourself or for someone you love who is battling anxiety."

ARLENE PELLICANE, host of the *Happy Home* podcast,
and coauthor of *Screen Kids*

"We need more honest stories like Jon's, stories that move us toward healing and hope. If you are in the midst of a dark or difficult season, the vulnerability and biblical insight of this book will give you words for the pain you are feeling. Most importantly, though, it will lead you to Jesus, our ultimate source of rest in every season and circumstance."

PATRICK AND RUTH SCHWENK, cohosts of the *Rootlike Faith* podcast, and
coauthors of *In a Boat in the Middle of a Lake*

"Decades of work in the human resources world have shown me firsthand that mental health struggles, especially anxiety, are real and increasing. People who find themselves battling these paralyzing feelings that disrupt their daily lives will benefit from reading *Finding Rest*. Jon has the rare ability to articulate clearly his journey with anxiety and OCD, creating invaluable insights for those in a similar place. This book should be required reading in the business world, so we can all become more understanding of hurting people."

TOM DARROW, founder and principal of Talent Connections

"In *Finding Rest*, Jon Seidl provides an honest, practical look at anxiety, faith, and life. Through his own struggles, Jon has discovered a biblical response to the challenges so many followers of Christ face. The church's approach to mental health has been incomplete at best, and this resource will better equip the body of Christ to walk alongside people with these needs."

SCOTT KEDERSHA, marriage pastor at Harris Creek Baptist Church, and
author of *Ready or Knot?*

FINDING REST

A Survivor's Guide to Navigating the Valleys of Anxiety, Faith, and Life

JONATHON M. SEIDL

KREGEL
PUBLICATIONS

Finding Rest: A Survivor's Guide to Navigating the Valleys of Anxiety, Faith, and Life
© 2021 by Jonathon M. Seidl

Published by Kregel Publications, a division of Kregel Inc., 2450 Oak Industrial Dr. NE, Grand Rapids, MI 49505.

The author and publisher are not engaged in rendering medical or psychological services, and this book is not intended as a guide to diagnose or treat medical or psychological problems. If medical, psychological, or other expert assistance is required, the reader should seek the services of a health-care provider or certified counselor.

The persons and events portrayed in this book have been used with permission. To protect the privacy of individuals, some names and identifying details have been changed.

Published in association with Cyle Young of C.Y.L.E. (Cyle Young Literary Elite, LLC), a literary agency.

All Scripture quotations, unless otherwise indicated, are from the ESV® Bible (The Holy Bible, English Standard Version®), copyright © 2001 by Crossway, a publishing ministry of Good News Publishers. Used by permission. All rights reserved.

Scripture quotations marked CSB have been taken from the Christian Standard Bible®, Copyright © 2017 by Holman Bible Publishers. Used by permission. Christian Standard Bible® and CSB® are federally registered trademarks of Holman Bible Publishers.

Scripture quotations marked NIV are from the Holy Bible, New International Version®, NIV®. Copyright © 1973, 1978, 1984, 2011 by Biblica, Inc.™ Used by permission of Zondervan. All rights reserved worldwide. www.zondervan.com. The "NIV" and "New International Version" are trademarks registered in the United States Patent and Trademark Office by Biblica, Inc.™

Cataloging-in-Publication Data is available from the Library of Congress.

ISBN 978-0-8254-4671-9, print
ISBN 978-0-8254-7721-8, epub

Printed in the United States of America
21 22 23 24 25 26 27 28 29 30 / 5 4 3 2

To my wife, Brett.
Without your encouragement, patience, sacrifice,
and sometimes frustration, no one would be
reading these words.

Come to me, all who labor and are heavy laden, and I will give you rest. Take my yoke upon you, and learn from me, for I am gentle and lowly in heart, and you will find rest for your souls. For my yoke is easy, and my burden is light.
—JESUS (MATT. 11:28–30)

CONTENTS

FOREWORD

I'VE KNOWN JON PERSONALLY AND professionally for many years. We've laughed, learned, and dreamed together. During that time I've come to understand his heart and his character. I've also come to understand his struggle with anxiety—a struggle that I know others deal with as well. (I've also come to understand why he's always so quick to return emails!)

As I've traveled the country for decades and talked with people at conferences and read the comments during our online fireside chats in my backyard, I've noticed an influx of people who are hurting and dealing with mental health challenges. Chief among them seems to be a struggle with anxiety. And in light of how the world changed in 2020, that has only increased.

So when Jon started talking to me about a book on anxiety and mental health, I knew how important it was. I also knew how uniquely positioned he was to talk about those topics. In *Finding Rest*, Jon has written something so special that others can't help but be drawn to it.

What I love about the conversation you're about to have in the ensuing pages is that Jon's words come from a place of profound experience. He's been there. He is there. He knows better than most what it means to battle anxiety and how to forge a path to victory. He also treats it with care and pushes the conversation to places that it hasn't often gone in the church. For example, he gently balances the spiritual and physical aspects of mental health, showing you how important it is to focus on both in order to find rest.

In that way, this book is unique. Instead of having to search out multiple resources on the topic, you can learn how to attack anxiety both physically and spiritually right here. I think that's invaluable.

As a bonus, this faith-filled guidance is beautifully written and, at times, funny. *Finding Rest* is the type of book that you read not only for the content but also for the way it is constructed. It's exactly what the church and her members need right now. Many of you know me as a student of history, and as I've learned through all of my studies, the writings of people who are genuine, faithful, and truthful will endure. I believe Jon's words here will endure for years to come. You'll find them encouraging not just the first time you read them but the second and third times too, as I won't be surprised if you return to drink from the book's deep well of knowledge.

If you're searching for peace, calm, and relief from anxiety, *Finding Rest* will help you find those, not just because of what the book focuses on but because of *who* it focuses on. True rest will never be found outside of the One who created it, and that person is Jesus Christ. Jon's found that to be true. I've found that to be true. And I believe, through reading this book, you will too.

I'm excited for your journey to begin—for what you will find and, most importantly, who you will find.

Godspeed,
Kirk Cameron

INTRODUCTION

TELLING THE WORLD MY SECRET

To say I planned on telling the world my secret would be a lie.

I didn't have some grand desire to reveal what I had only recently discovered but had been hiding ever since. It was January 2016, and I was working at a Christian nonprofit called I Am Second. If you don't recognize the name, chances are you'd recognize the work. They're the ones that use a white chair, a single overhead light, a dark room, and dramatic music to tell gripping stories of some of the most famous celebrities and athletes in recent memory, everyone from Clayton Kershaw to Chip and Joanna Gaines. The stories are intimate, deep, and personal. They are stories of hitting rock bottom, stories of immense pain, and ultimately stories of true hope.

It was being around those stories that I think led me to open up the way I did and tell my own. My role at the organization was to develop written content to publish between video releases, as well as to oversee any writing related to the videos: descriptions, marketing language, anything that would support and highlight the powerful stories. I cultivated a team of freelancers who were producing some

15

incredible content for us on our blog. One writer in particular got extremely vulnerable, talking about her depression, her loneliness, and even her suicidal thoughts as she navigated life as a young woman in New York City.* After reading and editing one of her stories, I was, I guess you could say, a little convicted.

Here you are asking other people to bare their souls, and you know you're holding out, I told myself.

So one afternoon I went for it. I didn't tell anyone beforehand, not even my wife. I just started writing. Words, thoughts, and ideas came flooding out. What resulted was the most honest piece of writing I had produced to that point. The title was just as honest: "It's Time to Tell the World My Secret." And here's how it started:

> We talk a lot about being real, raw, and relatable around the I Am Second office. I'm about to be more real and raw than I planned on being when I first started working here.
>
> As I sit here writing this, I'm a little tired. Not because it's 3:15 in the afternoon, but because I took my medication at lunch. My medication makes me tired. That's why I usually try to take it at night. And that's part of the reason there are days I go to bed at 7:30 p.m. (I say "part" of the reason because the truth is I also have an 8-month-old daughter who likes to get up anywhere from 4:30–5:30 a.m.)
>
> See, I have a secret that I've kept from a lot of people. I've told close friends and family. But I still have a fear about coworkers, bosses, and others knowing. I think the big reason is I don't want anyone to ever use the excuse, "Oh, that's just the _____ talking," or, "Oh, you're acting that way/feel that way because of the _____."
>
> But something has been happening lately. Karis Rogerson has been taking space on this blog to be vulnerable about her

---

* Having lived in New York City myself for nearly seven years, I can say that it is one of the most populated yet loneliest places in the world. It's so easy to fade into the background and become another unknown face.

struggles. She's incredible. She's inspiring. She's challenged us to talk about our problems so that they can't control us. And I thought it time to follow her lead. Likewise, the newest member of the I Am Second team, Caitlin McCoy, vowed to get really vulnerable with you. I respect that. A lot. And what better way to hold her to that than to put myself out there, too?

So want to know what medication I take? It's called Fluoxetine. You probably know it as its name-brand equivalent: Prozac. It's a popular antidepressant. I don't struggle with depression. (In fact, a lot of people say I'm one of the most joyful people they've met.)* But Fluoxetine can also be used to treat some other things. Those "other things" include anxiety and obsessive-compulsive disorder.

I have been diagnosed with anxiety and OCD.

You have no idea what's going on inside me right now admitting that to the world. To my bosses. To everyone I work with, have worked with, and will work with.[1]

I still feel a little something inside of me when I reread those words. Not fear, not dread, but emotion. Admitting you have anxiety and OCD, or any type of mental health issue, is terrifying. If I'm honest, every once in a while something happens that makes me wonder if it was the best decision. But then I'm quick to remember the reaction I received to telling my secret and those thoughts fade. Seriously, the emails, letters, and comments people sent me were so overwhelmingly positive that it makes every little twinge worth it. I had high school friends and acquaintances—the type you never expect to hear from again, the ones who seemed to have it all together—seek me out to tell me about their own struggles and thank me for giving them a voice. Complete strangers were messaging me in droves, even contacting my

---

* Those words about not having depression were written before I, well, had depression. And before I understood that "appearing happy" wasn't a way to ward it off.

wife and asking for her advice on how to help a loved one who is struggling.*

The most stunning response was from a stranger named Jason.

"You're probably never going to read this, but I think this article saved my life," he wrote on Facebook. "Not really sure how to say thank you."

It's hard to put into words what reading that did to me at the time. What it still does to me. And from there, the comments kept pouring in:

> Thank you so much for sharing your story. There are many, many of us who struggle through depression/anxiety and other issues and take meds, and sharing your story helps us feel we are not alone in secrets.

> Your stories mimic mine. But I failed myself by stopping my meds because I didn't want to feel broken. I want to thank you for your honesty and vulnerability in posting your struggles. It was an awakening for me.

> I was so afraid to call my anxiety what it was for so long. . . . I thought that medicine was a crutch and I should have control over my own mind enough to overcome those feelings. I kept it hidden from everyone and spent a good amount of time in emotional agony in search of the root of my problem. . . . Thank you for taking the time to share and own your feelings, it's really important to talk about that stuff and I just want you to know how much I appreciated it!

> Wow! Everything you mentioned in the I Am Second article is me to a T. . . . I've never talked about these things to anyone. I really thought it was just me. My dad is a pastor so a lot of this stuff I feel like I can't share. Thanks for showing me I'm not alone.

---

* This was a huge motivation for including that advice in chapter 9 of this book.

While I was encouraged by those comments, I was also heart-broken. The common thread in a lot of them was that the person had a mental health struggle, was a Christian, felt immense shame, was told that faith would "cure" them, and had zero support from their church or faith community as they fought their battle. Their families just didn't understand what they were going through, medication and seeking help were demonized, they were restless, and they were alone. Many of them felt like the only way to get through their struggle was to hide it, ignore it, or deny it. In other words, they had to keep their secret inside. And I could relate. I felt many of those same things, and if not for the overwhelmingly supportive environment I found myself a part of at the time I came out with my secret, I'm not sure I ever would have been open about it.

And that's why you're reading this now. I want to tell your story by telling my story. I want to help you by putting into words what it's like to be so confused and frustrated by what's going on in your head that you retreat for hours, days, or sometimes years. I want to explain how you can address both the physical and spiritual aspects of what's going on inside you and still have a deep and rich faith. I want to give family members who have been searching for answers some sort of relief and lifeline. I want to help the church better understand how to care for the members of the flock who have been misunderstood, misguided, or ignored. I want to help all of you finally get in the open what has been taboo and hidden. I want to show you how to take care of yourself. I want to help you understand what it means to take advantage of the common graces God has given us as tools in this fight.

I want to help you find rest—the type of rest that comes from understanding what's going on inside of you, being understood by others, and knowing how to fight back with practical tools to overcome the disorder.*

But ultimately I want to help you understand why this is happening

---

* We'll clarify this more, but know that "rest" doesn't mean a complete absence of your difficulties. I recently had surgery, and even though I was struggling with pain, I was still able to find rest during recovery.

and how God is still working in the midst of it. I want to help change your view of what it means to have faith during the trials, and even undo some of the harm that's been done to you in the name of God.

In other words, this book is meant to be used as a battering ram to break down physical, spiritual, and relational walls when it comes to mental health. It's for the person who struggles with anxiety and OCD and has built barriers around themselves, either intentionally or because they're confused by what's going on inside them.* It's for the family member of that person, so they can learn how to empathize with their loved one and help tear away the layers of helplessness that often plague those forced to wade through the secondary effects. And it's for the church, which needs to be challenged to remove the thick stigma surrounding mental health and be Christ in real, hands-on ways to members who feel ostracized, lost, and hopeless.

This book is also meant to go deeper than I've ever gone while giving you practical and spiritual truths that you need to embrace, breathe, and live. The stories I tell feature new admissions that I've never talked about publicly. The truths are rooted in the only thing that has sustained me through the driest deserts and darkest valleys of my life: the gospel of Jesus Christ.

⌒

I come from a line of short people. I'm five foot six. My mom is four eleven. My sister is four eleven. My great-grandmother, as far as I can tell from pictures, was four eleven. My grandpa? Five foot five on a good day.

But my wife, Brett? Now, she's the complete opposite. She's at least five eight, and much taller in heels. (You should see some of the funny looks we get when we're on a date.) Her dad is well over six feet. Her grandpa? The same. Old pictures of her grandma reveal a stunning woman with "legs for days," as people like to say now. By the looks of

---

* We'll also talk about depression, though that is not the main focus.

it so far, my young daughter got her mom's genes. Unfortunately for my son, however, his height is about as Seidl as it comes.

Why am I telling you this? Because I want you to know that I am extremely honest about who I am. I am a short, stout man with cocktail weenies for fingers. I don't run away from it. I don't hide from it. I'm not ashamed to admit my shortcomings* and weaknesses. I'm a little overweight, although as you'll read, I'm working on that for a variety of reasons. I find certain clothes I like and I wear them too much because I don't like wasting mental energy on picking out an outfit. I didn't go to school to be a writer. Instead, I went to college hoping to be the next press secretary of the United States of America. I fell into journalism by accident after discovering during a freshman writing class that I was kinda good at it. And I have anxiety and OCD.

I tell you who and what I am—even down to the small details—so you can trust me when I tell you what I'm not. I am not a psychologist. I am not a doctor. I am not a clinician or a counselor. I am not a pastor. I am not the traditional "expert" on anxiety and OCD. I don't have a PhD or a theology degree hanging on my wall. I have a Packers flag. I have not written thousands of pages of medical research, but rather thousands of stories about everyday life. This book is one of those stories, and it's written from a place of both deep struggle and profound understanding. Let me be clear: you, the reader, are not who I *was*; I *am* who you *are*. What I mean is that victory in this battle against anxiety and OCD doesn't mean I no longer have obsessive thoughts, it doesn't mean I don't have panic attacks, and it definitely doesn't mean I'm immune from experiencing new battles, like the depression I never saw coming. The difference between you and me is that I'm telling my story and what I've discovered along the way. I hope by the end of this book, even that difference will disappear as you become more comfortable talking about your struggles.

When it comes to mental health issues, I write from a place of deep personal experience and, yes, pain. Have I done my research to better

---

* See what I did there? I'm also a sucker for a good (or bad) pun.

understand myself? You bet. Remember, I have OCD, so I've probably gone a little overboard. Have I talked with professionals about it?
Absolutely. Am I the subject's leading expert? Please, no. What you're
about to read isn't from the mind of someone crafting peer-reviewed
journal articles on the topic. It's from the mind of someone who, like
you, many times can't shut it off.*

For example, as I write this, it's 9:14 p.m. on a Tuesday night. When
I woke up this morning, I had no intention of tackling this introduction. But as the day went on, I had an idea. That idea turned into
something I couldn't shake, and now my mind won't stop until I get
it out on paper. In many ways, this is the blessing of OCD. I don't let
things slip through the cracks, and once I put my mind to something,
I get it done.

But here's the thing: I don't ever want you to trade what I'm saying for the help I've found in seeking guidance from professionals.
Think of this book as a long talk with a friend—the kind of friend who
understands what you're going through and can talk to you about it
over a rich cup of coffee, a tall glass of wine, or a cold beer. After you
and I talk, I need you to take the next step and go even deeper with
your community, mental health professional, or pastor.

In other words, I want you to use this book as a supplement or
maybe even a jumping-off point. While my journey with anxiety
and OCD started long before I got professional help, the process of
fully understanding who I was only started once I allowed people far
smarter and wiser than I am to begin speaking into my life.

This book isn't meant to cure you. In fact, I don't consider myself
"cured" just because I have named and understand what is going on
inside of me. But I do consider myself whole, because I'm approaching
my disorder holistically and drawing closer to Christ as a result. That's
what I want you to do. That's a concept I'll explain in depth later, but
suffice it to say that I'm more than content to be a guide who turns
your gaze inward so you can understand yourself, outward so you can

---

* Rest assured, though, this book has undergone a theological review.

realize how you affect and are affected by others, and upward so you can find the true source of rest. That's what I want you to take from this. Don't give me one ounce of credit more than that.

Read this book to find hope. Use it to get help. Embrace it to find rest.

CHAPTER 1

CALL IT BY ITS NAME

A FEW YEARS AGO MY wife, Brett, and I had brunch with a group of friends from our small group at our church in Texas. It was the first time we had gotten together in a while, since kids and babies had started replacing game nights and cocktails.

As we sat there wrangling our children and making ridiculous deals with the toddlers to get them to take one more bite of their food, one of the women broke the news: "We're pregnant!"

Cheers went up and hearty congratulations poured out. I'm not sure I have ever heard so many high-pitched "Ahhhhhs" in my life. Then something interesting happened. After someone asked the inevitable questions of "When are you due?" and "Do you know what it is?" a third question quickly followed: "Have you picked out a name?"

The couple had, but they slyly refused to tell us. It drove everyone nuts. We asked if we could guess, and when they said yes, it began a twenty-minute interrogation with every name possible being thrown against the wall to see if it would stick. (Think of a classic version of the game Guess Who breaking out in the middle of a packed restaurant. "Does this little person start with a *D*?") I even went deep into the Bible and threw out Tryphaena and Tryphosa. No dice. Finally, after a few hints we coaxed out of the couple's two-year-old, I guessed it: Charlotte. The screams for us figuring out the name were just as loud as when we got the baby news earlier. The tables near us cheered a little too, as by then they had become secretly invested in figuring out the name as well.

So here's the question: why is that? Why are we driven, seemingly inherently, to ask about a name? Why do we *have* to know what something or someone is called? The answer, in true *Beauty and the Beast* fashion, is as old as time.*

For starters, it gives us control. In ancient Jewish culture, there's an idea that if you can name something, you have power over it. Think back to the garden of Eden. After God gave Adam dominion over the earth, Adam took on the task of naming every living thing. By naming them, he was in a position of control over them. When we name something, we own it. We take responsibility for it. We even protect it.

But names have another purpose beyond ownership and control. They allow us to communicate properly about whatever the thing or person is. They allow us to categorize it. They allow us to understand it. There's an exponential level of knowledge that comes with knowing someone or something's name. It can tell us so much. It's why our group of friends wanted to know the baby's name. Knowing her name would open up a whole new world of insight. In this instance, it would lead to a deeper understanding of the parents by then talking about why they chose that name, asking why it was important to them, and discussing things like family heritage.

We see this emphasis on names throughout the Bible. Moses longed to know the name of whom he was talking to in the burning bush. Jacob, while struggling with the stranger on the shore of the Jabbok River, asked for the assailant's name. The angel gave Mary Jesus's name—Emmanuel—when he appeared to her and announced the coming of the Son of God. Matthew spends seventeen verses on the

---

* This reference is almost solely in honor of my young daughter.

names in Jesus's genealogy, while Luke spends fifteen doing the same thing. That's a lot of names.

We want to name, and we want to know names. Only then, it seems, can we properly appreciate whatever it is. Only then can we understand it. Only then can we face it. The absence of a name—the unknown—is not only a powerless place but also a place of deep confusion.

That's how you could categorize a lot of my teen and young adult years. For twenty-seven years of my life, I had no idea what was going on inside of me—I didn't have a name for it. I was confused. I was angry. I was upset. I was frustrated. I had feelings I couldn't put into words. And I could never seem to turn off my mind.

Why do I feel this way? Why can't I stop thinking about this? What am I so worried about? What's the worst that could happen? (Don't answer that!)

My brain always seemed to be racing. Like a dog chasing its tail, it would go around and around and around . . . and around some more. Only, in those earlier days, I think a dog had a better chance of catching its tail than I did of slowing the exhausting cycle in my head.

My first "episode," as I recall it, happened when I was twelve. My mom, one of my sisters, and I were in our white Dodge Caravan pulling up to our country home in Wisconsin. Our house was set back about three hundred yards from the road, and the routine we had for getting the mail looked like Mom stopping at the end of the winding gravel driveway and one of us kids hopping out and walking to the mailbox situated right off the shoulder. Because of the Badger State's perpetual cold, my siblings and I would always argue over who had to make the mail run. On this day, I drew the short straw.

I pulled open the sliding door and ran toward the mailbox. After I grabbed the letters and various magazines, I brought them back and started thumbing through them. As the result of adding my name into some spammy internet pop-up, it wasn't odd for me to come across something with my name on it. But as I surveyed the mail I didn't see anything for me. That's when the thought, like one of those time-lapse videos of a flower opening in the morning, began slowly spreading in my head.

You aren't important. No one seems to care. You're not even special enough to receive a piece of junk mail.

I remember it vividly. I can still feel the depths of defeat and woefulness that welled up inside, all over a lack of mail. It all came out of nowhere, like some dark, secret part of my brain had just been unlocked. I can still hear the voices. And I can remember the conversation as those voices traveled from my head to my throat along some invisible highway of lies.

I turned to my sister. "Well, Jenny, it looks like you got something. I didn't. No one seems to care about me. No one seems to think I'm special enough to even send me something. When's the last time you even got something for me, Mom?"

Where is this coming from? I remember thinking. I had no idea, but it just kept coming. If I close my eyes, I can still see the perplexed looks on both Mom's and Jenny's faces.

"Jonny, what are you talking about?" my mom said.

"Well, I just don't seem to matter to anyone. Sometimes I don't seem to matter to anyone here either," I replied.

"Jonny, stop it," my mom said somewhat dismissively. That only fueled the thoughts even more.

"I'm serious," I said. "Everyone else gets things in this family, but everyone forgets about me."

We pulled up to the house and all got out.

"Jonny, you know that's not true," my mom said as she shut the door.

Deep down I did. But by that point it was too late to pull myself out of it. The dog had darted from his kennel and was in full tail-chasing mode. I spent the rest of the night unable to convince myself to stop thinking the thought I didn't want to be thinking. It was that night that I first remember turning to a coping mechanism I would use for years in order to shut off my mind. I imagine you've probably found some sort of method too.

That mechanism involved a long-held dream of mine. I have always wanted to be in the FBI. The idea of being a federal agent chasing serial killers, criminals, and terrorists still excites me. I even took the FBI entrance exam several years back and passed, and if not for an injury to my shoulder that required surgery, you might not be reading this book right now.

On the night of that first episode, I lay in bed unable to think of anything but the "no one cares about me" lies in my head. It was exhausting. I was so tired but unable to sleep. That's when I reached into the only part of my brain that didn't seem to be controlled by the uncontrollable thoughts: my future glory with the FBI. To tune everything else out, I started creating a movie in my head where I was the star special agent. Where I mattered. I imagined what it would look like for me to burst through the door of some serial drug dealer and lead a raid that brought him to justice. It granted me the relief I so desperately needed. That scene—and a few more after it—played in my head until I fell asleep. Soon it became one of the only ways for me to find relief at night from my own mind. In other words, the only way to get a reprieve from my racing thoughts was to replace the unwanted ones with others that were just as furious but more palatable. Go figure.

But finding a way to cope was different than understanding what was going on inside of me. From that day on, I remember easily getting fixated on things. A girl, an idea, a thought, a comment from someone else, a fear, and especially a worry. Those thoughts would consume me. I remember looking at classmates in high school who lived more carefree lives than I did and it made me jealous. Not in an "I hate them" kind of way but in an "I want the relief you seem to have" kind of way. Imagine how confusing that was for a young Christian who was always told that if I followed Jesus and did the right things, others would want what *I* had.

Secretly, I never understood why anyone would want whatever this was.

For twenty-seven years of my life, to varying degrees, that was my reality. I never knew why. I never could figure out why I just couldn't "get over it," whatever "it" was. That continued on through the early years of my marriage. Brett would do or say something and I would stew on it, replaying it in my head like some slow-motion, high-definition video and dissecting it into a million little pieces. It was slowly driving a wedge between us as I turned to other coping mechanisms like work, alcohol, and porn to try to find relief from the unceasing thoughts.

Then in 2014, the epiphany happened. It produced a name.

⌒

At the time, Brett and I were living in a loft in downtown Dallas. The bottom floor included a hip coffee shop we frequented, complete with reclaimed wood tables, concrete pillars, local art, and a stage in the corner for open mic nights and B-list musical acts. You know the type.

But for everything the coffee shop had going for it, there was one big deficiency. See, I like Sweet'N Low in my coffee (the pink stuff), not real sugar, not stevia, and especially not Splenda. The coffee shop stocked the pink packets from time to time but not on a regular basis. It was more of a Splenda place, which to me tastes a little like bitter sock water. I just gagged a little.

On this day, a Saturday I think, we decided to go on a walk around downtown. But first we needed our coffee. Brett took care of the drinks while I ran to the bathroom. I went out of my way to remind her that I wanted Sweet'N Low in it. If they didn't have any, I wanted it black. When I returned, I took a sip of the coffee and I almost spit it out. It was disgusting. It was awful. It was full of Splenda. I can't describe what happened in my brain. I didn't get enraged and lose it like a madman. But a rush of anger, disappointment, and "Why couldn't you do this one simple thing?" flooded over me. I didn't want to feel that way. I remember even telling myself, "This is not a big deal!"

But it was.*

---

* Before I ever even had her read my first draft of this book, my wife suggested the title be *I Just Want My Sweet'N Low*.

My wife told me to get over myself. That's always been a trigger for me, so it just made it worse and threw me into a bad cycle, like when my mom told me to just "stop it" that day in our driveway. I walked out and left her alone in the coffee shop. Our day was ruined. Seriously. For the rest of the day I couldn't get over her putting the wrong sweetener in my coffee and then telling *me* to get over it. It was awful.

We didn't talk about it for the rest of the day. In fact, we didn't talk at all. The next morning, she expressed how helpless she felt. She was confused and hurt. The term "walking on eggshells" got used a lot as she reminded me this wasn't the first time. There were frustrated tears.

"Jon, your reaction was not normal," she said. She was right. It was my normal, but it shouldn't have to be hers. I apologized and told her I thought I needed to get help. I knew this wasn't right. It wasn't something she should have to endure. There were more tears, not just from her but from me. And even though she forgave me, she made me commit to getting some sort of help.

That's when I called my sister, who I knew had sought help for her mental health and had seen a psychiatrist. I explained to her what was going on.

"Jess, this is probably going to sound either really weird or really normal, but I have to tell you what happened," I said. As I told her the story, she chuckled. I remember thinking, *Why are you laughing?*

"Oh, Jonny, you definitely have it. Don't you know it runs in the family?" The "it" was anxiety and OCD.

No, I didn't.

She proceeded to rattle off all the family names like some kind of biblical genealogy. She gave me examples of her own struggles, like how she would get upset with her husband if he didn't mow the lawn a certain way. Hearing her say that triggered so many memories. I started thinking about my own examples.

Like how sometimes when cleaning the house with my wife, I would get inexplicably annoyed if she wasn't doing it in a certain order. "The floor before the dishes? Why?" Seriously. She would ask, "What's wrong? Why do you seem so upset?" It caused so much strife in our marriage.

I thought about how I would regularly reread emails (especially ones I sent) upward of fifty times, convinced there was an error I was missing or an unwanted tone I was accidentally communicating that I didn't pick up on the first forty-nine times. If I only read it one more time, I would finally be able to relax. That was rarely the case.

At times I would lie in bed at night, convinced I didn't lock my car. I would wake up at three in the morning with the locked-not-locked scenario in my head, get up, stumble through the living room, go to the car, and check the door. It was always, of course, locked.

I thought about all the things I just couldn't let go, like when my wife once scraped the car bumper during a minor parking-garage fender bender and I obsessed over it for a week. I could not stop thinking about it.

How much is this going to cost? Why does this happen whenever we get nice things? Why couldn't she see the other car? What's this going to do to the trade-in value?

I remembered the time I was driving to the grocery store. At the intersection, I heard a thump underneath my car. Any normal person would have thought, *Oh, I just ran over a piece of trash, or maybe a squirrel,* and not even given it a second thought. Me? I drove to the store and couldn't shake the feeling that I had run over not just something but *someone.* On my way home before I pulled into the driveway, I retraced my route. Not once, but twice (literally three minutes later) to make sure. I was looking for blood, for emergency vehicles, for people taking pictures. I still thought I had missed something when I got home. That scenario happened numerous times.*

The conversation with Jess was an epiphany moment—so much made sense now. It was a relief. Scary, but still a relief. I hung up with her and immediately scheduled a doctor's appointment for the first psychiatrist in the area who had an opening for new patients. I needed

* The second title Brett suggested for this book? *I Thought I Ran Over a Human, but It Was Just an Ant.* She's got a great sense of humor. That said, one comfort I received when I finally told the world what was going on with me was that other people shared how they had this same fear of running over someone. It's not a completely uncommon worry among people with anxiety and OCD.

to find out if I did, in fact, have anxiety and OCD—and what I could do about it.

_⌒_

To say I obsessed about the appointment a lot over the next couple weeks would be an understatement. It continued through the day of the appointment. I remember sitting in the waiting room of the doctor's office, which was situated in a high-rise overlooking a major Dallas freeway.

What if he tells me there's nothing wrong with me?
What if he says I'm overreacting?
What if there's nothing he can do?
What if . . . ? What if . . . ? What if . . . ?

Ironically, the fact that I was obsessing so much over the questions was an answer in and of itself.

When the doctor—who looked like a slightly more polished version of Doc Brown from *Back to the Future*—finally called me in and asked me to tell him why I was there, my heart was racing. My mouth, which was as dry as the Sahara, could barely catch up to my brain. I'm already an excessive sweater, and I could feel the droplets forming everywhere. *Everywhere.** Somehow I managed to give him the examples that came to mind while on the phone with my sister. He nodded and took notes on a yellow legal pad. He started saying things that felt like he had cameras in my apartment, going through other scenarios and asking if I had struggled with any of them.

"Yes!" I remember shouting at one point, with my face and palms turned upward. "Thank you!"

Then the moment came. He smiled. "You have what's called generalized anxiety disorder with obsessive-compulsive disorder, OK?" He then explained what that meant.

At that moment, I almost broke down in tears. Not because I was

---

* One thing I've come to realize is that excessive sweating is a symptom of anxiety. It's caused by the fight-or-flight response the body goes through.

sad, but because I was so happy. I was relieved. I was overjoyed. I felt known. The terms *anxiety* and *OCD* didn't make me feel helpless. They made me feel powerful. I was finally able to name and understand what was going on in my head, in my relationships, and in my day-to-day life. I was finally able to make sense of who I was for the past twenty-seven years.

⌇

Since then, I've come to understand exactly what anxiety is, and with each discovery my world gets bigger. One of those discoveries is important to mention here. It relates to the interplay between anxiety and OCD. I have both, but not everyone does. It's like one of those classic word problems from school: all those who have OCD have anxiety, but not everyone who has anxiety has OCD. That's because OCD is a type of anxiety. It's a subset. That said, if you struggle with anxiety, it's not odd to have OCD tendencies.

"The struggle with obsessions and compulsions is a struggle with anxiety," explains Mike Emlet of the Christian Counseling and Educational Foundation. "Anxiety is the heart of this problem."[1]

In other words, I have anxiety, and my obsessive-compulsive disorder is the unhealthy way in which my brain tries to deal with that anxiety. Why tell you that? Because I want you to understand that even if you don't specifically struggle with OCD, everything I'm talking about here is still for you because the heart of the problem is something we share.

⌇

If you're reading this book, you've either named your own struggle or are on the path to doing so. Maybe you've struggled with anxiety for years, or maybe you realize something is "different" or "off" and you're looking for answers. I'm glad you're here. There is power in calling who you are and what you have by its name. It's biblical. It isn't a sign of weakness. It's a sign of strength. Only after you name it can you begin to understand how to fight back and overcome.

Just ask my friend Noah. Like many people, he started experiencing anxiety seemingly out of nowhere during the coronavirus pandemic of 2020. About a year earlier, Noah had moved his family to Amsterdam for his job. They had barely settled into what life would be like as foreigners in a country they knew little about when the virus hit and upended everything all over again. Toward the end of April, at the height of the spring lockdown, he had to travel to Germany for work. That's when the fear and anxiety set in. Had he been nervous before? Sure. But this was different. This wasn't normal. This was something bigger. He is normally a calm, mild-mannered man. But the anxiety began transforming him into someone on edge, with severe heart palpitations and profuse sweating. And frankly, that was both confusing and paralyzing.

That's when he paused, took a step back, and really examined what was going on. That's when he realized what the issue was: he was having full-blown, raging anxiety attacks. It scared him a little to admit it, but he did.

"I don't think I knew what to call it at first," he texted me. "But now I am mature enough to admit it: fear, anxiety, and lack of control."

Admitting what was really going on led to freedom. Why? Because by recognizing and naming what was going on, only then could he properly address it. He was able to seek guidance, to draw closer to the Lord, and to find some answers. The almost debilitating fear of travel, the cycle of thoughts about "What if?" and the fear of the unknown that haunted him all dissipated only after he knew what he was facing. In other words, only after knowing how to ask the right questions was he able to find the right answers.

See, owning your diagnosis prevents your diagnosis from owning you. That's what I'm hoping you find in the coming pages. Hope. Hope that you don't have to be controlled by what seems uncontrollable.

Like what happened with Noah, so much in my life made sense to me once I was able to put a name to what was going on. It helped me understand why I quit football—my passion since I was in fifth grade—as a high school junior (I had a raging fear of failing). It helped me realize why it had become so easy in college to fall into a porn addiction that lasted through the first few years of my marriage, despite waking up every day wanting to stop (obsessive thoughts and pictures more easily embed themselves in my brain). And it helped me understand my family history and some of their actions that had caused confusion in my life (it was hereditary).

But naming it also did something else. It started me on a journey that would give me a better understanding of all of my life's difficulties, as well as a clearer understanding of who God is and what He's up to.

That may not make sense at this point, but it will. I firmly believe that my anxiety and OCD can, have, and will be used for my good and God's glory. Whether you've named your own disease yet or not, I think you will too, by the end of this book.

CHAPTER 2

THE MOST IMPORTANT BOOK OF THE BIBLE

IN THE INTRODUCTION I MENTIONED I had a Green Bay Packers flag hanging on my wall. It's special to me. It's important to me. It's a big part of who I am. I got the flag from the team's victory parade after they won the Super Bowl in 2011. The temperature on that February day in Green Bay was in the single digits and I had flown from New York City, where I was living at the time, just to be in Wisconsin with my family to watch the game. After they won, I extended my trip so I could be a part of the celebration. It was worth every nearly frostbitten toe. And I'd do it again in a heartbeat.

Why do I tell you that? Because my (somewhat unhealthy) love for the Green Bay Packers led to one of the most important discoveries of my life. It's a discovery that happened even before I was able to name what was going on inside me, and it showed me how God is working in—and redeeming—my pain, my frustration, and even my mental health struggles.

It's also how He's redeeming yours.

The Minister of Defense

I'll never forget where I was on December 26, 2004. I can even tell you the cross streets and intersection. At the time I was a senior in high school. It being Christmas, I was spending time with family, and on this particular day I was driving in the car with my stepdad, Mike. We were stopped at a light in front of an old 76 gas station that had a sign for "two-cent Tuesdays," which meant all senior citizens could get two cents off each gallon of gas when they filled up. There was a break between songs on the radio, and that's when the DJ delivered some shocking news: Reggie White, the great Packers defensive end, was dead. We'd learn later it was due to complications from sleep apnea.

I couldn't believe it.

Not only was White one of the greatest players to ever wear a Packers uniform, and not only did he restore glory to the storied Packers franchise by helping us* win the Super Bowl during the '96–'97 season, but he also had a unique nickname: the Minister of Defense. It was a title given to him because of his outspoken faith, as well as his status as an ordained minister that he obtained at age seventeen. In fact, he would regularly deliver special sermons at the church he attended in Green Bay, and after retirement he became a pastor in North Carolina.

His wasn't the type of Christianity that simply thanked God at the end of a good game. He lived it. He embodied it. After winning the Super Bowl with the Packers in January 1997, he told *Sports Spectrum Magazine*, "I think God showed me that there is more to life—to let the whole world know about Jesus. I think that was even bigger than winning the game."[1]

The man was incredible. He loved God. He lived for Jesus. He died in tragedy.

So imagine my shock when Mike started shaking his head after hearing the news and said, "You know, that's really sad. But it's even more sad because Reggie must have had unrepented sin in his life."

---

* Yes, I said "us." That's how we talk about the Green Bay Packers. After all, the fans own the team. No lie. The team has shareholders.

"What do you mean?" I asked, not only shocked but utterly confused. I had heard rumblings of this concept at my childhood church but never really understood what it meant.

"Don't you know the Bible promises us seventy years, Jonny?"* White was forty-three. "He must have had something he hadn't repented of."

I got angry. This was one of my idols. I would watch highlights of his Super Bowl season before every single one of my own football games, sometimes twice.

"You've got to be kidding me, right?" I asked disgustedly.

"Do your research," Mike snapped back. From there, the conversation deteriorated, with me saying how ridiculous I thought that was, and Mike telling me how I needed to be more "in the Word" to understand.

I left that interaction angry and in disbelief, but also with so many questions. Some of them are the basic questions that any young person exposed to tragedy begins to ask, like, "Why do bad things happen to good people?" But others were deeper:

- Are we guaranteed to live seventy years?†
- Am I at risk of dying tomorrow if I'm not constantly—like every minute—asking for forgiveness for my thoughts and actions?
- If I need to constantly be asking for forgiveness, then why was everyone telling me that Jesus already died for my sins and paid the penalty on the cross?
- How soon do you have to ask Christ for forgiveness after doing something wrong before you are no longer at risk of dying from it?

---

* The idea comes from Psalm 90:10, which says, "Our days may come to seventy years, or eighty, if our strength endures" (NIV).

† The answer is no. Billy Graham in 2005 responded to the idea that this verse means we are "promised" to live until at least seventy: "God wasn't promising that every person would live to be seventy or eighty, however; the psalmist was simply describing our normal human experience." See Billy Graham, "Does the Bible Say Somewhere That God Has Promised to Give Us 70 Years of Life?," Billy Graham Evangelistic Association, February 22, 2005, https://billygraham.org/answer/does-the-bible-say-somewhere-that-god-has-promised-to-give-us-70-years-of-life/.

- Is God keeping score of my good and bad deeds and ready to unleash some sort of tragedy to put me in my place?
- What type of unrepented sins leads to you being struck down in your sleep?

As the questions mounted, so much of what Mike said at the time didn't *feel* right, but I didn't understand why. I didn't have anything concrete to base that on. So I took the challenge he offered me that day. From that moment on, I started a process to "do my research" and figure out why I disagreed so much with what he said.

And that's when I found the book of Job. Over the next few years, this one book would change my life, my outlook, and my faith.

"Blameless and Upright"

The book of Job is forty-two chapters long and sits right before one of the most popular books of the entire Bible, Psalms. As a quick overview, it follows the story of a man named Job who is described as "blameless and upright, one who feared God and turned away from evil" (Job 1:1). Talk about an intro. You can't get any better than that, right? I mean, basically the guy is everything you ever want to be. That's what makes the story so powerful. Despite the fact that Job was such a great guy, his world was rocked by all sorts of tragedy. He had ten kids—they all died. He had three thousand camels, five hundred cattle, and five hundred donkeys—they all died. He was a healthy man—and he *almost* died.

A big part of the book is Job and his friends trying to figure out why this is all happening to him. Job's friends take a position that was so eerily familiar to me. They tell Job that he needs to repent because he must have done something wrong to cause all his pain and suffering.[*]

The reader knows from the beginning this isn't the case. Job isn't experiencing tragedy because of anything he did. He wasn't living in

[*] In the end, it's for Job's friends that the Lord reserves the biggest rebuke: "My anger burns against you . . . for you have not spoken of me what is right, as my servant Job has" (Job 42:7).

sin. He wasn't hiding something. He wasn't unrepentant. In fact, the book tells us that Job lost almost everything and was on his deathbed not because he was responsible for any of it but because God had a plan. See, God allowed all these things to happen to Job because He wanted to prove something to the devil. The devil told God that Job only worshipped Him when, and because, things were going well, and if He took away all of Job's wealth, family, and livelihood, Job would curse God.

God took the bet. While He didn't directly *cause* Job's suffering (He didn't author it, the devil did), He *allowed* it to happen. He let the devil do whatever he wanted to Job, as long as he didn't kill him. And while Job was confused and distressed, he never cursed God, just like God knew he wouldn't.

But even though Job didn't curse God, he still got upset. He asked questions, like where God was during all of this. Those questions— along with the fact that he raised them—are crucial, because how God responded gives us one of the most beautiful, poetic, and stirring explanations of why tragedy is not a simple cause-and-effect relationship and why we can't always understand His ways. Here's that response, which includes God using some questions of His own:

> Where were you when I laid the foundation of the earth?
>   Tell me, if you have understanding.
> Who determined its measurements—surely you know!
>   Or who stretched the line upon it?
> On what were its bases sunk,
>   or who laid its cornerstone,
> when the morning stars sang together
>   and all the sons of God shouted for joy?
>
> Or who shut in the sea with doors
>   when it burst out from the womb,
> when I made clouds its garment
>   and thick darkness its swaddling band,

and prescribed limits for it
   and set bars and doors,
and said, "Thus far shall you come, and no farther,
   and here shall your proud waves be stayed"?

Have you commanded the morning since your days began,
   and caused the dawn to know its place,
that it might take hold of the skirts of the earth,
   and the wicked be shaken out of it?
It is changed like clay under the seal,
   and its features stand out like a garment.
From the wicked their light is withheld,
   and their uplifted arm is broken.

Have you entered into the springs of the sea,
   or walked in the recesses of the deep?
Have the gates of death been revealed to you,
   or have you seen the gates of deep darkness?
Have you comprehended the expanse of the earth?
   Declare, if you know all this. (Job 38:4–18)

In other words, God's explanation for why He allowed Job to go through all the pain and suffering was: because I am God. His ways are not our ways. He sees the whole picture when we see a fraction of it. It wasn't because of something Job did or because God was angry at him. It was because God had a bigger plan and a bigger purpose in mind. In fact, in Job 1:8 it's *God* who mentions Job to the devil. God is the one who asks the devil if he had noticed Job, thus setting the whole story and chain of events into motion.

That's in stark contrast to what Mike claimed to me that December day in the car. In that view, there's always a direct link between our current suffering and our past actions, or even our right actions and our lack of suffering. Reggie White died a tragically young death, therefore Reggie White absolutely did something wrong to cause it.

That's not what's in the book of Job. That's not to say our sinful actions don't have consequences or directly affect our future. The meth addict is gambling with his life every time he plunges the needle in his arm. The alcoholic risks a DUI whenever he gets behind the wheel drunk.* But Reggie White wasn't a meth head or a drunk. He was a pastor. His situation was like Job's, not a junkie's.

As I read the book, and reread it numerous times, not only did it blow my mind but it also felt like a cold glass of water on a scorching hot day. It was refreshing, life-giving, and sustaining. It was my aha moment. My faith made so much more sense. My feelings that day in the car made sense. I had finally found an answer to the questions that spun in my head for years. My view of God was radically changing, and it was almost euphoric.

Reggie White didn't die from sleep apnea because he had unrepented sin. Reggie White died because the devil is still working to destroy, because there is evil, sin, and brokenness in the world. It's around us, it's in us, and it's among us. One of the effects of that evil is a fallen world, and in a fallen world, tragedy happens. Yet, all of that still happens under the watchful eye of a loving God. Could He stop every evil thing from happening? Could He abate all tragedy? Of course He *could*. But He doesn't. Some He allows. Why? Well, that doesn't always make sense to us. It can't. But Job shows us that it has to do with using our struggle for our ultimate good and His ultimate glory.

Our Good

The phrase "for our good and His glory" is important to understand. It's foundational to this book and to my understanding of why I struggle. It's going to come up a lot, so I want to take some time to explain it.

Let's start with the first part: "for our good." How do we know for sure that our struggles are something God is using for our good? Job

---

* I think one of the most tragic elements of being human is that while we see and experience the tragedies God doesn't prevent, we forget that we can't see, or will rarely ever see, the ones He does prevent, like the addict who doesn't die from an overdose or the drunk driver who doesn't collide with an innocent family. Doesn't God deserve the credit for abating those tragedies?

himself tells us. In Job 42, at the end of the book, he spells it out: "I know that you can do all things, and that no *purpose* of yours can be thwarted" (verse 2, emphasis added). Later he adds, "Therefore I have uttered what I did not understand, things too wonderful for me, which I did not know" (verse 3). Read that again. Job's trials brought him to a place of complete surrender, a place where he recognized that God is sovereign, that we can't always understand what He's doing or why He's doing it, and that He has a *purpose*, even if it's unknown to us. At the risk of sounding trite, he's learned that God is God, and we must trust Him even if we don't understand what He's doing in the moment.* That understanding, that type of spiritual maturation, is ultimately the best thing for Job—it's for his good. It's better than any possession he lost and more important than anything he will ever gain.

That brings us to Paul. Romans 8:28 is a verse many churched people can recite by heart (even if they don't know the reference). It goes, "And we know that in all things God works for the good of those who love him, who have been called according to his purpose" (NIV). Paul lays out in one verse what it took Job an entire book to understand: God is working all things for our good. How can we know that our tragedies and our pain are going to be redeemed? Because God tells us that's exactly what He's going to do. My anxiety and your anxiety may be some of the most difficult things we ever experience, but we have hope because God says He's going to use them for our good. It's what He promises. That should comfort us, not confuse us, especially when we can't figure it out. It's like the moment in every thriller where someone inevitably tells the protagonist, "I have no idea how your plan is going to work and how we won't all die, but I'm just going to trust you."

A word of caution, though. It's important to understand that we are not the arbiters of what is good. We don't decide what's in our best interest. If you know the story of Job, you know that at the end the Lord restored Job in such a way that he ended up with more children, animals, and possessions than before. Double, actually. The temptation,

---

* I have found, though, that as time passes I frequently can look back and see what God was up to.

then, is to think that's what it always looks like, that because Job got *more* that's how God worked everything out for his good, and that's how He's going to work it out for our good too. But that interpretation glosses over the real meat of the book of Job. If you look at Job 42, the mention of Job's fortunes being restored comes across as more of a footnote. It's a part of the story, sure, but it's not *the* story. The most important thing Job gained is found in the first six verses of the chapter that I mentioned earlier; it's his deeper relationship with and richer understanding of God. The possessions are just the cherry on top. I'm here to tell you that sometimes the best thing for us is that we don't get the health, the wealth, or the relief.

Yet too many times we define good as something that makes us feel better, or as the absence of anything bad. We look at Job's restoration and demand that our "good" has to mean a doubling of our possessions, better circumstances, better health, or more money. Or in our instance, no anxiety. But that's not what we see in the Bible. You could pick almost any stalwart of the faith and see that many times their *ultimate* good had nothing to do with something physical and everything to do with something spiritual. Their struggles pushed them closer to God and gave them a deeper understanding of who He is. *Because* of the hardship, they gained the ultimate good, which is God Himself. It may be hard for us to see how something like the death of someone close to us or our mental health struggle can be used for good, but we know from Job and from Romans that it will be, many times in the form of a deeper relationship with the One our soul deeply craves.

That, friends, is truly good news.

His Glory

So what about the "His glory" part of the phrase? It can be a confusing topic. But it's definitely not a foreign one. When Jesus heard that His friend Lazarus was sick, His first response was, "This illness does not lead to death. It is for the glory of God, so that the Son of God may be glorified through it" (John 11:4). What does that mean? Remember, I am not a theologian or a seminarian. But let me explain what I've come to understand about how our struggles bring God glory. I think we get a massive clue in Isaiah 48:10–11:

> Behold, I have refined you, but not as silver;
>   I have tried you in the furnace of affliction.
> For my own sake, for my own sake, I do it,
>   for how should my name be profaned?
>   My glory I will not give to another.

Why does God allow us to go through "the furnace of affliction"? To refine us, for one. But also "for my own sake." And what is the sake of God? To be glorified. In other words, our refining brings us closer to God, and the closer we get to God, the more we reflect His glory. In the commentary on verse 11 in the English Standard Version study Bible, it says, "The deepest motive in the heart of God is his own glory, to the exclusion of all other glories."[2] We talk a lot about how God is love, which is true. But we don't talk enough about how God's glory is also paramount to who He is and what He is about. Yet it is. In fact, we are told that in everything we do we are to bring Him glory (1 Cor. 10:31). It's also, not surprisingly, what we were created to do. The first question in the Westminster Shorter Catechism asks what our chief purpose is. The response? "Man's chief end is to glorify God, and to enjoy him forever."[3]

While not much in life can be reduced to a simple formula, I think in this case there's a benefit to trying to reduce this down to one:

- Our struggles, our refining, bring us into a closer relationship with God.
- By being closer to God, we glorify Him more.
- When we glorify Him more, we are fulfilling what we were created to do and what He seeks most.
- Therefore, our struggles have a tendency to be not only for our good but also for our best, as they help us to fulfill our ultimate purpose: glorifying God.

That's the beauty of what happened with Job. Even though he was blameless (Job 1:1), he still had room to grow closer to his Creator, and his struggles made sure that happened. Likewise, our tragedies have a way of forcing us to Christ, creating a deeper relationship between Him and us. As that happens, we reflect more of His glory, and ultimately that's what a holy God deserves and wants—and it's what we were created to do.

I'm not saying the concept of God being glorified in our struggles isn't a little mysterious. After all, Lazarus did suffer a physical death in order that God, through Christ, would be glorified, and that can be hard for us to wrap our minds around.* But faith is filled with mystery. This is a mystery we're called to accept (see 1 Peter 2:23, 4:19; and 2 Cor. 12:7–10). The way Pastor John Piper sums it up helps me: "God is most glorified in us when we are most satisfied in him."[4] That word *satisfied* brings me a lot of comfort. By striving to bring God glory I am drawing closer to rest, contentment, and satisfaction. Isn't that so much of what we find ourselves striving for here on earth anyway?

Applying Job to My Anxiety and OCD

The story of Job, as well as the lessons from it, has been revolutionary for me. One of the biggest and most practical takeaways is that it helped me make sense, at the deepest levels, of why I was struggling with anxiety and OCD. In short, it provided the proper context to understand my mental illness.†

Because of the way God reveals Himself in the book of Job, I don't see Him as a type of Dr. Frankenstein who is cobbling me together

---

* Still, you could argue it was for Lazarus's ultimate good: he died, but he was then raised to life. It's also a beautiful foreshadowing of our life in Christ. Even though we die, we don't experience the ultimate effects of death. We are raised into the presence of God, and that is better than anything on this earth. The beauty of being a follower of Christ is that in death we actually experience a new life. That's for our good . . . and His glory.

† I sometimes shrink back a little bit from calling it "mental illness." In society today, "mental illness" is what mass murderers and psychopaths have—or so I've told myself. But then I remember that one of my goals and one of the goals of this book is to *erase* the stigma. So let's boldly call it what it is: mental illness. That's OK. That doesn't mean you're on your way to a straitjacket and a locked ward.

with misfit internal and external parts. He didn't curse me with mental illness, and He definitely didn't give it to me as a punishment for something I did wrong. Quite the opposite. Remember Moses at the burning bush? He started pointing out all his deficiencies and inadequacies when God was calling him to lead His people out of slavery in Egypt. God's answer?

"Who has made man's mouth? Who makes him mute, or deaf, or seeing, or blind? Is it not I, the Lord?" (Exod. 4:11).

You know what that means? I can rest in the fact that nothing happens without God knowing, that it is ordained by Him, and that if I'm struggling He is using it in a bigger, deeper way. The fact that He has ordained the storm is not a cause of anger or fear. On the contrary, it's a comfort. Because that means, in His wisdom, He knows what He's going to do with it and use it for. The great hymn writer William Cowper once wrote, "Behind a frowning providence He hides a smiling face."[5]

My anxiety and OCD aren't for nothing. On the contrary, He's redeeming them and using them to bring me into a deeper relationship with Jesus.

I've gone back and read Job several times since my diagnosis. And as a result, there are three main takeaways that I keep coming back to that I think are useful for all of us who struggle with all forms of anxiety. However, and here's the beauty and grace of God at work, these also apply to *any* type of difficulty:

1. Job provides us with a proper understanding of the gospel.
2. Job gives us a rich picture of who God is.
3. Job offers a framework to understand why we as Christians still encounter difficulty.

Let me take those in order, because they build off of each other. First, the gospel of Jesus Christ is that there is nothing I can do to make myself better or more worthy of God's love. I can't "earn it." It's not about simply repenting "enough," or putting myself on a strict confession schedule so that God doesn't send hardship into my life. That was what I heard from Mike. Instead, God loves me not because of what I do, but in spite of it. It doesn't change. My circumstances aren't a reflection of whether or not His love is true and real.

Even Job himself, a man God called "blameless and upright," couldn't secure guaranteed health and prosperity by being blameless. In fact, right before God answers Job, we are introduced to a young man named Elihu. Part of what Elihu does is chastise Job for even hinting that because of all the good things Job's done in his life, he's not deserving of the suffering he's going through (see Job 35). While Elihu's rebuke isn't completely spot-on, there's still an important lesson in it: we can't curry God's favor by being good. I really want that to sink in.

Second, God isn't some accountant with a well-worn, backroom ledger keeping track of every good and bad thing I do, and when the bad overtakes the good He's not just waiting to send something along to punish me. Does God allow immediate course corrections in our life? Yes, we do face discipline at times. But even then, it's meant for our ultimate good. He's not some rottweiler on a leash just waiting to bite us the moment our "bad deeds" column outgrows our "good deeds" one. If that were the case, we wouldn't make it much past two years old before the guard dog of heaven tore us to pieces. Remember, God's greatest rebuke in the book of Job was reserved for his friends who claimed his circumstances were the result of something bad Job had done (see Job 42).

And third, it is promised that we are going to experience suffering, tragedy, loss, hurt, and pain. Someone once pointed out to me that the most powerful, awesome, and amazing people of the Bible all experienced pain. David, Abraham, Paul, Peter, Esther, Job, the list continues. So if the people we're supposed to draw inspiration from dealt with tragedy and difficulty, what does that say about what I can expect? Never mind that Jesus Himself made it clear: "In this world you will have trouble" (John 16:33 NIV). Hardships are unavoidable. And even though Job was "blameless" he still suffered immense hurt and pain.*

As those takeaways became clear, I started to apply them to my specific struggle. It went something like this:

1. There's nothing I can do to make myself worthy of God's love, and there's nothing I can do to force Him into giving me what I want. My decision to follow Christ has to come with an understanding that I am powerless to entice His favor. I have done nothing to earn His love and there is nothing I can do to make Him stop loving me. Nothing I think, nothing I fear, nothing I do, can separate me from Him (Rom. 8:38–39). I must love Him and follow Him because of that, not because of what He may or may not do for me or give me. I must love the giver and not His gifts.

2. My OCD and anxiety are not God's punishment for anything I've done. They're not judgment for being mean as a young child, for not being the "best" Christian, or for struggling with a porn addiction. I can't get rid of them by treating repentance like some A + B = C Excel formula: if I believe in God (A), and ask for forgiveness on a regular basis (B), then God will take away what I don't like (C). I can do nothing that requires Him to give me what I want (perfect health) and prevent what I don't want (anxiety and OCD). While I can still pray and ask that He take them away, there's no guarantee that He will. If He doesn't, I have to understand that He is still good.

3. My anxiety and OCD exist because we live in a fallen world. Bad things happen, disease spreads, and mental illness is a reality because sin entered the world. But because God is good and

---

* Once again, where did we get the idea that "blessings" are only the things *we* deem to be good for us? That's so absurd! If I only got what I thought was good for me, my life would be miserable. If you have kids, you know exactly what I mean. My daughter wants candy constantly, but I know it's not good for her. So sometimes I have to do things that are for her ultimate good, even if in the moment she doesn't appreciate it.

powerful, He doesn't leave us alone. He takes what is meant for evil and works it for my good and His glory. While my anxiety and OCD are here because of the sin that entered the world, I can still have hope for redemption and sanctification through Christ, a hope that I know can only be truly fulfilled outside of this world, while still fulfilling my calling to endure in this one (Rom. 5:1–5).

It's the same conclusion drawn by C. S. Lewis. Second to the author of the book of Job, the writer who has had the greatest effect on me is Lewis. I named my son after him (Jack, as J. R. R. Tolkien and others called him). Lewis not only lost his mother but also his wife, leading to some of the most raw and insightful words on pain and suffering ever penned. Did Lewis ask questions of God like Job? Of course. But in the end he reached the same conclusions: pain and suffering—and death, for that matter—while difficult, are being used by God for our ultimate good and His ultimate glory. In Lewis's case, that good was to show him exactly what he believed and *why* he believed it.

"God has not been trying an experiment on my faith or love in order to find out their quality," he writes in chapter 3 of *A Grief Observed.*[6] "He knew it already. It was I who didn't. In this trial He makes us occupy the dock, the witness box, and the bench all at once. He always knew that my temple was a house of cards. His only way of making me realize the fact was to knock it down."

Sometimes God allows us to be knocked down in order for us to realize that only by reaching up for Him can we ever stand again, and to help us understand that God is God and we need to approach Him not for what He can give us, but because we can never fully be whole and complete unless we rest in Him. Our trials have a way of making us realize how small we are, how big God is, and how desperately we need Him. Even Paul was given a thorn in his flesh "to keep me from becoming conceited" (2 Cor. 12:7).

In the same chapter of *A Grief Observed*, Lewis employs an analogy that explains it perfectly. He uses the example of playing cards and betting money, and how raising the stakes (or upping the ante) forces us to show how much faith we have in our hand:

> You will never discover how serious [your belief] was until the stakes are raised horribly high, until you find that you are playing not for counters or for sixpences but for every penny you have in the world. Nothing less will shake a man—or at any rate a man like me—out of his merely verbal thinking and his merely notional beliefs. He has to be knocked silly before he comes to his senses. Only torture will bring out the truth. Only under torture does he discover it himself.[7]

In other words, our trials have a way of forcing us to admit whether we truly believe what we believe. We can say all we want that "God is enough," but we will never truly know if we believe that until we're forced to live it out. That's why I call Job the most important book of the Bible, because it is a fundamental explanation of who God is and what our relationship to Him should be. We get a front-row seat to how Job learned that. After lobbing question after question at God, demanding an answer for his tragedy, Job finally got an answer from God. God didn't explain *why* Job went through it, but rather explained that He—God—is all-powerful, all-knowing, and all-seeing. That was it. How did Job respond? He rested in that. When Job was on his apparent deathbed, the answer he got to why he was suffering was, "I am God. That's all you need to know." And you know what? That answer quickly became good enough for Job. And if it's good enough for Job, it has to be good enough for us. The question we should have for God isn't, "Why have you allowed this to happen?" Rather, it should be, "What are you using it for?"

Discipline Versus Punishment

Your anxiety, your OCD, your mental health struggle is not God punishing you. Rather, it's God pursuing you. It's Him allowing you to experience, in a most beautiful way, how greatly you need Him and how strong and faithful His love is for you. He is purifying you, using all things in your life, even your anxiety and OCD, to discipline you and make you more holy.

Wait, by using the word *discipline* did I just contradict myself and say He's punishing you? Nope.

See, we don't do a good job of distinguishing discipline from punishment these days, but it's a crucial distinction, especially for Christians.* Our minds, for some reason, automatically think of punishment when we think of discipline, and not only is that unhelpful but it's also flat-out wrong. Punishment is retribution for a past wrong. It's a penalty. When you think of it, you think of anger and wrath. You think of shame, guilt, and fear.

But that's not discipline. Discipline is about training. It's about correcting. It's soft. It's gentle. It's not angry. It's not retribution.

Think about it in the military sense of how marines are trained to *have* discipline. When they arrive at boot camp, they have a lot of old habits and old ways of thinking that need to be changed. They are put through rigorous training to create new habits and new instincts. The point is not to make them pay for something they did. It's not punishment.

As a sinner, I can definitely say that I often struggle with wrong thinking, selfish desires, and whatever else you want to group with those. That's my bent. I need discipline, then. I need it often. You know what? I have seen clearly and vividly how God uses my anxiety to turn me toward Him in those moments and in those seasons. When I try to do everything on my own, when I forget how much I need Him every day, my anxiety throws me into His arms. When I become consumed with my own thoughts and alienate those around me as a result, I have nowhere left to go but to Him. In other words, my struggles often show me how much I am in need of someone to control my

* This is a really great sermon on God's sovereignty and how, in some instances, that involves discipline: Afshin Ziafat, "The Discipline of Our Heavenly Father," Providence Church, January 12, 2020, https://www.providencefrisco.com/mediaPlayer/#/sermonvideo/429.

life and how often I neglect to turn to God. It shows me how much I need His discipline.

And God is faithful enough to do that. He's faithful enough to use my anxiety and OCD to prove how much He loves me, how much He cares for me, and how present He is in my life. That's why Hebrews 12:7 says that we should "endure suffering as discipline" (CSB). It's not a discipline like an angry parent flying off the handle at their teenager for doing something wrong. Instead, it's done in a loving, caring way that has your future good in mind. It's discipline that forces you to lean into Him more and to experience His grace to meet you in your every need. Here's how Piper puts it: "There is an infinite and precious difference between God's retributive justice in punishment and God's purifying discipline in our pain. That difference does not lie in the origin, the human origin of the pain—whether good or evil. It lies in the purpose and the design of God in our suffering."[8]

Once again, He's allowed your mental health struggle—He's using it—to refine you, grow you, and ultimately use you. Punishment is cause and effect. Discipline is grace-filled. It's hopeful. It's helpful. That's incredible news!

Making Sense of It All

I've done a lot of looking back not only on my overall struggles but also on specific valleys that have been especially dark. And as the Lord has been taking me on this mental health journey, I can tell you my perspective is different now than it was at the beginning of all this. I can genuinely say I am thankful for all that's happened—the anxiety, the OCD, the depression, the struggles, and the reactions.

Why? Because all those struggles, battles, and disappointments have forced me into a deeper relationship with Christ. They have forced me to admit that I can't figure out any of this on my own. They have forced me to admit I can't control everything. They have forced me to admit I need something and someone greater.

Paul Miller in his wildly popular, wildly necessary book *A Praying Life* talks about using our anxiety as "a springboard to bend our hearts to God."[9] It's a great visual when you think about it. A springboard bends down, flexes, and is at its greatest point of stress right before it propels you toward where you need to go. Not only do we gain power over something when we name it, but imagine what we do to it when we actually use it to propel us—like a springboard—closer to the One who can make sense of it all. It takes on meaning. It takes on purpose. Our goal becomes something more important than just making it all stop.

Charles Spurgeon is credited with the saying "I have learned to kiss the wave that throws me against the Rock of Ages."* It's the same thing Miller is saying, but said much more poetically. That doesn't mean you won't get a little beat up by the waves, by the way. After all, have you ever tried to kiss a wave? But it does mean that whatever trials are thrown your way, you can be thankful for them when they push you into a deeper, more abiding relationship with Christ. Once again, God is certainly not the author of evil. He didn't cause my anxiety, my OCD, or my depression. But He is faithful enough to use the bad, the difficult, and the hurt in our lives for our good and His glory. That is something we can be thankful for.

It's why James tells us that we should "count it all joy" when we face trials (1:2). The use of the word *joy* and not *happiness* shouldn't be overlooked. It's not talking about a momentary feeling but rather a bigger, healthier perspective on what those trials are doing—they are bringing us closer to Christ. It's the same thing we see in Romans, where Paul tells us that "suffering produces endurance, and endurance produces character, and character produces hope, and hope does not put us to shame" (Rom. 5:3–5).

Which brings me back to Spurgeon.

Spurgeon is more than just a famous preacher from the 1800s. He

---

* What Charles Spurgeon said in his 1874 sermon "Sin and Grace" was, "The wave of temptation may even wash you higher up upon the Rock of ages, so that you cling to it with a firmer grip than you have ever done before, and so again where sin abounds, grace will much more abound." See "6 Quotes Spurgeon Didn't Say," Spurgeon Center, August 8, 2017, https://www.spurgeon.org/resource-library/blog-entries/6-quotes-spurgeon-didnt-say/.

is often called "the prince of preachers." His messages are some of the most read and quoted among people of all denominations. He's a titan of the faith. And yet, did you know that he struggled with his mental health? He had an ongoing battle with depression. In fact, it was such a struggle that he and his wife wrote openly about it. He even gave advice to young preachers not to be surprised if they found themselves full of "melancholy."[10]

Spurgeon, the "prince of preachers." And yet he struggled with depression. So when he talks about kissing the wave "that throws me against the Rock of Ages," those aren't empty words. It's advice from someone who has been fighting the mental health battle and found the only way to make sense of it all is to turn to Christ.

You know what that means, right?

Pucker up.

Mike's Reaction

Let me say this unequivocally: I love Mike. The effect my stepfather has had on my life has been deep and profound. Sure, there are things we disagree on, but the love he has offered my siblings and me from the moment he stepped into our lives is beautiful. He's also been willing to listen to me over the years. In fact, since that conversation in the car, Mike and I have had many conversations about sin, about God's promises, and about the Christian life. He has evolved in his thinking. As a result, Mike has apologized for what he said that day in the car and we have subsequently grown closer. I attribute that to the work of the Holy Spirit as well as God's continued faithfulness to use tragedy to draw us closer to Him.

One tragedy in particular seemed to change his perspective. That was the death of my thirty-two-year-old sister, Jenny, in 2018. It helped him see things differently. It was hard for him and for all of us. And just when I thought God had taught me all He was going to teach me with her death, tragedy struck again and He made sure I understood.

But more on all that in the next chapter.

CHAPTER 3

THE FOUR DEATHS

THIS CHAPTER IS BY FAR the most emotional thing I have ever written, yet it is one of the most significant. Why? Because head knowledge is important, but heart knowledge is what sustains you. My wife, Brett, tells couples that we meet with for premarital counseling that there will come a time when they have to live out their vows in real and practical ways. Those times are generally not fun. They are messy, and they are often marked by heartache.

What you're about to read is how I was challenged to live out everything I had come to understand about suffering and tragedy. Did I really believe God is working all things for my good and His glory, or was that just head knowledge? It was going to be put to the test. If you want to understand what you truly believe and if you truly believe it, death, as C. S. Lewis found out, has a way of clarifying those things.

My Grandparents

I have a vivid memory from my childhood. It goes like this.

I'm in the middle of the backyard of my grandparents' house sitting at a white, wrought-iron, miniature picnic table set. The house has real wood siding that's painted blue with white accents. The backyard is massive, because the house sits on a double lot, and large maple trees tower above us as the sunlight and their leaves cast shadows on our faces. There's some sort of snack in front of me as well as a drink. I'm maybe five or six. My grandma is across from me, while my grandpa is piddling around doing some sort of nonessential busywork near the back patio. Our goal is simple: listen for the low rumble of an airplane, and then wait for the wind to peel back the leaves revealing the winged wonder. I can still hear the drawn-out Midwestern *o* and *a* in my grandma's "whoa" whenever our little quest proved successful.

There were a lot of those types of moments growing up, vivid and wonderful memories featuring my grandparents as key figures. To say my grandparents helped raise me feels too flippant a way to describe what they meant to my childhood. My parents divorced when I was three. During and after that time, I would spend long stretches at my grandparents' house, most times unplanned, sleeping next to my grandpa with one of his oversized T-shirts as my pajamas. When things were tough at home—which was often, as my stepdad, Mike, was thrust into fathering four kids the day he married my mom, and the youngest of my two sisters, Jenny, started showing signs of addiction early in her teens—I would call them and, without asking questions, whichever one was available would immediately hop in their car, drive outside the city limits where we lived, and usher me into some sense of peace and normalcy. When the chaos got really bad, I would sneak out onto the roof of the house and wait, hoping to get a better view of them making the turn into our winding gravel driveway—eagerly anticipating the relief they were bringing.

When I went off to college, my grandma would faithfully send me ten dollars every month, always stuffed in a card with a note.* "I know it's not much," she would say every time. She'd repeat that when I called her, because when I got the card, I was expected to (and gladly

---

* She knew that for five dollars I could get my favorite lunch, General Tso's chicken, from a hole-in-the-wall Chinese place that was eventually shut down by the health department. She would tell me that at least it was good for a couple of lunches.

58

did) check in on her and Grandpa. It could have been one dollar and it would have meant just the same to me.

In every sense of the word, they were *grand*parents. I told you that my anxious episodes started in my childhood, and in looking back I spent a lot of time with my grandparents because being with them meant I was away from circumstances at home that fueled my episodes. Because of Jenny, my home life was chaotic, it was frantic, and it was both physically and emotionally loud. She was angry and frenetic and was prone to some of the most unimaginable screaming fits. But at Grandma and Grandpa's house it was so quiet I could literally hear the sound of an old clock ticking. No noise. No yelling. No drama. Just peace and quiet.

And yet in a situation I consider ironic, it's likely that the anxiety and OCD I struggle with to this day is something I inherited from my grandma. It wasn't diagnosed, but it didn't have to be. She worried endlessly, mainly about her health. Her doctor knew her very well. There seemed to always be something she was going to see him about. She was particular about the smallest details. She wasn't mean about it, but she let you know. There was a bathroom in her house no one but she could use. The drapes had to be a certain way, and only select people could operate them. The grandkids were chastised if they touched the walls going up the stairs. She was religious about her schedule. There are many words to describe her, and anxious would be near the top of the list.

In October 2013 she gave us a scare. She got really sick, I don't remember from what, and she ended up in the ICU. It wasn't looking good. I caught the first flight to Wisconsin from Texas and prepared myself to say goodbye. I cried the whole way there. But somehow, someway, she pulled through. I couldn't believe it.

Four years later, we weren't so lucky. In January 2017, after another trip to the ICU and a bout of pneumonia, she died. She was the matriarch of our family, where the women generally have big personalities and have never succumbed to dated stereotypes. Her presence was irrefutable when she was alive, and that made her absence that much more noticeable.

While I was hurting, my grandpa was something much worse: heartbroken. Although they bickered like two squirrels from time to time, especially near the end, they loved each other deeply. When I went to visit him one last time before returning to Texas after Grandma's funeral, he looked down and mumbled, "I can't believe she left me."

Three months later to the minute—to the minute—he died. While it's become cliché to say he died of a broken heart, in this case it is the best way to describe what happened. A fall put him in the hospital, but once there he didn't have any fight in him. Without Grandma, he lost the will to live. He wanted to be with her again so bad, and he couldn't wait to be reunited. He got his wish.

In the end their deaths weren't unexpected. Grandpa was ninety-four and Grandma was eighty-seven. They lived long, full lives. So while I have never struggled with why they died, I have struggled with their absence. In fact, there are times I still ugly cry (another term I guess they say these days) because I miss them. I remember one time not too long ago, my young daughter, Annie, found a picture of them from our wedding and brought it to me.

"Daddy, this is your grandma and grandpa from Wisconsin, right?" she asked. "You loved them a lot. Do you still miss them?"

I broke down right then and there. Yes, yes, I do.

They were my rocks. But as I said earlier, death has a way of making you look back and evaluate. In their deaths, especially my grandma's, I was reminded of something important: God can still use you despite your struggles.

I said it was pretty obvious my grandma struggled with anxiety and OCD. Despite all of that—despite her worries, her schedule, and her particularity—she loved me well. Isn't it just like God to use someone who struggles with anxiety to offer comfort and stability to someone else struggling with anxiety? Isn't it just like God to take someone who internally may be going a hundred miles per hour and make her home the place of peace and refuge for someone going a thousand miles per hour? That's been incredible for me to realize and think about. It's been amazing to know that despite *my* own struggles, I can still be used by

God to help others in a similar way. In fact, over the last five years Brett and I have had four different people live with us, all generally coming from chaotic situations and looking for relief. They found refuge in *my* home, the home of a person who struggles with anxiety and OCD. Yeah, God is still using you despite your struggles.

I can read for hours about how God loves me and is taking care of me, but only after losing my grandparents and sitting in the hurt and reflecting back did I see the awesome way in which He used them to show me how He's using me today.

My Sister

I will never forget the guttural, almost animalistic screams I heard that night. The first ones came from my oldest sister, Jess, the second from my mom.

I was driving on the George Bush Turnpike in Dallas on my way to a screening for Clint Eastwood's movie *The 15:17 to Paris*. I had gotten an invite to a special prerelease screening ahead of an interview I had set up with the real-life heroes on whom the movie was based. I was able to bring a guest, so I asked my friend Corey to join me. I hadn't known him long, but after meeting him through church I thought this would be a good opportunity to connect. We were chatting in the car when my phone rang. It was Jess. I remember thinking about whether or not to answer. I didn't want to be rude to Corey sitting next to me, especially considering this was a "man date" of sorts. But my mom had been dealing with some health issues recently and I didn't want to ignore the call in case it was an important update. That fear was about to become reality, but not in the way I expected.

"Hey," I said, putting her on speakerphone. If you've watched the Netflix series *Making a Murderer*, you know that we Wisconsinites tend to answer the phone with one-word, pithy greetings. I know, it's a little weird.

But I wasn't met with the response I was accustomed to. Immediately the screams started pouring out like I was talking to some sort of gasping, hyperventilating teenager.

I was able to make out a few disjointed words. *Gone. Accident. Interstate. Dead.*

"Whoa, Jess, slow down! What? What happened? Who?" I asked, and probably shouted. I could feel my anxiety welling up. Something was wrong. My heart started racing as the adrenaline kicked in.

Trying to calm herself but failing miserably, she took a few choppy breaths—the kind of breaths you take when you're crying hysterically. Finally, she found some sort of momentary respite. "Jenny was in a car accident. I just got a call from someone saying she was on the interstate and there was some sort of crash, and they think she was in it and she died." That's all she was able to get out before the wailing resumed.

"Do you know for sure?" I asked.

"Not really," she said before immediately breaking down again. In my gut, I knew the answer.

I told her I would quickly call our brother Jeremy—the oldest of the five siblings—to try to figure out what was going on, since I knew I could count on him to be more rational. She made me promise to call her if he told me anything. I said I would and hung up the phone, my heart racing even more as my head started spinning. I exited the turnpike and pulled my truck over on the side of the off-ramp. I dialed Jeremy's number and waited for him to answer.

"She's dead," he said as soon as he picked up the phone.

"What?" I asked in disbelief.

"She was in a car accident and was killed. The cops just came and told me." I'd find out later that the police came to where he was coaching his high school basketball team, pulled him out of the locker room during the pregame speech, and delivered the news in the hallway.

"We're on our way to Mom's house right now. Don't tell her anything until we get there." He was very short.

I said OK and we hung up. I stared at the dashboard as Corey placed his hand on my shoulder. Silence. But I was quickly jolted out of the moment by my phone ringing. It was my sister again.

"Jonny, did he tell you anything?" she asked hurriedly. I didn't know the best way to put it, so I just said it.

"Jess, she's gone. The police just met with Jeremy and told him." My voice cracked and I started crying.

"Noooooooooo!" she screamed in a way that chilled me.

And as if that wasn't bad enough, I heard another voice on the phone that wasn't supposed to be there. It was my stepdad, Mike.

"Jonny, did you say she's dead?" he asked. I was caught off guard.

"Yeah . . . yeah, that's what Jer just told me," I said.

"She's dead," he repeated, his voice cracking too. That's when I heard it. The most chilling sound I have ever heard and will ever hear. The sound that still haunts me to this day.

"No, no, no, no, no! Naaaaaaaaaaaaa! Ahhhhhhhhhhh!"

It was my mom screaming in shock and agony.

"I'm sorry," I said. "I didn't know Jess had put me on a three-way call. Jer is on his way over there with the police and a pastor." The screaming continued in the background.

"OK, OK," Mike said in a weak, shaky voice. "I need to comfort your mamma."

We hung up and I looked over at Corey.

"I'm so sorry, man," he said.

"She's really dead," I said, once again locking my eyes on the faint orange glow of the dashboard.

A few months later, we would get a full picture of what happened that day.

At about 3:25 p.m. a man in his truck and pulling a trailer parked at a building supply store in my hometown of about thirty-two thousand people. He bought some sweets and at least one bottle of aerosol-based compressed air, the kind you use to clean your computer keyboard. He immediately got on the interstate. After a few miles, something happened and he crossed the median, never slowing down and swerving into opposite-way traffic.

At the same time, Jenny was in a van with an elderly gentleman who had taken her under his wing. He was a retired railroad worker, and he was good at fixing cars. On this particular day, he had offered to take my sister to a local junkyard to get a new transmission for her vehicle that had broken down. They were on their way back when they encountered the man pulling the trailer at about seventy-five miles per hour.

The collision was absolutely horrific. The coroner sent me a disk of pictures. While he didn't include photos of Jenny's body, there were plenty of the scene itself. The van she was in was unrecognizable. Her side of the vehicle took the brunt of the crash, not just flattening it but disintegrating it. In one of the photos I could see her leg and boot peeking out of what was once the passenger door. She was thirty-two when she died. That's the same age I was when I first started writing this. That's sobering.

There are plenty of emotions that followed the events of January 25, 2018. Disbelief. Pain. Grief.

Her oldest child, a daughter named Emily, was fifteen, a time and age when you need your mom the most. In fact, her sweet sixteen birthday was just two weeks away, Valentine's Day.

That led to a lot of questions too, especially in the immediate aftermath.

Why her?

Why our family?

Why did my parents have to go through this?

Why, when she has three kids?

But the more time that has passed, the more I've learned from the entire ordeal, and God has been faithful to show me some important things. The most significant lesson? There's a difference between questioning God and asking God questions.

Asking questions is natural, it's normal, and it's expected. But questioning God is something greater, bigger, deeper. In essence it's doubting that He is good, that He is able, that He is capable of turning all these things for my good and His glory. Questioning Him cuts to the core of who He is and who we are. But asking questions in light of Jenny's death in many ways reassured me *more* of who God is, not less, and what He's doing.

Asking the questions brought me closer to Him. Asking the questions reminded me that He is present in our difficulties and our sufferings, in our pain and our diagnoses. While it was a difficult time, there was still something in my soul that made me turn to Him to make sense of the pain. The answer I got to all my questions was that He would use this tragedy for something bigger. And if He's faithful to use something like this for good, then certainly He's faithful to use my own struggles—including my mental health ones—for good as well.

His faithfulness amid Jenny's death became clear to me as I thought back to standing in the receiving line at her casket and shaking hands with hundreds and hundreds of people.* As I remembered their faces, I also remembered their backstories. That's when I began to realize that as a result of Jenny's death, these people of all races, backgrounds, and degrees of "messed up" sat through some of the most gospel-centered eulogies and messages of hope they'd probably ever heard.

The service lasted several hours. Person after person shared about what it looks like to be a sinner in need of grace. They shared about how even though Jenny's life was difficult, confusing, and at times frustrating, she was more than the sum of her mistakes and tragedies. She was loved by the One who mattered most, even if she frequently forgot that. It was powerful. As I reflected on what was said, it became clear to me that there was something bigger at work. In short, I got a glimpse of what God was doing.

The response we got from people afterward confirmed what God was up to: Jenny's death allowed Him to reach more people than she ever did in her life—a whole college auditorium full of them. It was beautiful.

There are still questions that I ask God from time to time, like why He didn't intervene. I ask Him why the kids have to grow up without their mom. I ask Him why my mom had to and has to go through such grief. I haven't gotten an exact answer to all those questions. I may never. But the questions aren't bad. They're healthy. The more

---

* This isn't an exaggeration. We had to rent out a university auditorium for the funeral, and the hundred-year-old funeral home told us it was the largest funeral they'd ever been a part of.

I ask them, the more I'm forced to recognize that there is only One who can comfort me, and in asking the questions I am drawn closer to Him.

Job asked questions. David asked questions. Paul asked questions. It's not wrong to ask questions about your struggles, about your tragedies, about your mental health. Ask them. In asking Him your questions, you're acknowledging that He is there. When you acknowledge that He's there, you have to remember that He is at work, even if you have to wait a little longer to see exactly how.

My Stepdad

April 2020. Many will remember it as the height of the first wave of the coronavirus pandemic. But our family will remember it for something even darker.

I had recently started using my digital media background to help my church with tech and video projects, so when the pandemic hit I quickly became an integral part of our weekly video services once they went completely online. I was editing the Good Friday service, staring at a computer in our church sound booth with all the lights off for some reason, when I got the text.

"Did Jer call you?"

It was from my sister, Jess, and she was talking about my oldest brother, Jeremy.

"No, why?" Instantly a pit formed in my stomach, and my anxiety kicked in. My mom's health was still not great, and Jess had been struggling with deep depression since Jenny's death. I was concerned for both of them. Almost instantly my phone started ringing. It was Jess. What she said is the last thing I expected.

"Mike was taken to the ER this afternoon. He came home from work sick, woke up vomiting all over the floor, and called someone to take him to the hospital. When he got there, he lost consciousness and hasn't woken up since."

If a men's magazine did a story of the sixty fittest men over sixty, my stepdad, Mike, would be in it. He's not overweight; he eats healthy, clean, and organic; he still goes for runs on the beach; and he drinks enough water to make a fish jealous. Other than kidney disease at a young age that required a kidney transplant from his sister twenty-five years earlier, his health is perfect. Impeccable. He even completely weaned himself off his antirejection medication after his surgery, so his immune system isn't compromised in the same way as many other transplant patients' are.

In other words, he's the last person I expected to hear was in the hospital and unresponsive.

Jess proceeded to tell me that they were running tests as fast as they could. They had done a CT scan that was inconclusive, and they were stumped. Immediately I thought about COVID-19. She said they hadn't ruled it out and were actively testing him for it. The test would take days to get back. So until then we were supposed to wait.

The worst part? We couldn't see him.

What many people overlook or forget about the coronavirus pandemic is the havoc it wreaked on the families of those in the hospital. The measures being taken at care facilities were so comprehensive that those with family members in the hospital were not able to visit—especially if the patient was in the ICU, which Mike was.

But my mom was persistent. She begged and pleaded, and eventually the hospital made a concession to allow her and some select people in to see him as long as they geared up head to toe in personal protective equipment: mask, gown, and gloves. They stayed by his side as long as the nurses would allow, but he still didn't respond.

That night I got another text: "They put him on a ventilator." He could no longer breathe on his own. Later they tried to take him off of it, and his body made no attempt to take a breath. I didn't need the doctors to tell me what the prognosis was, but they told us anyway. An MRI revealed Mike had a massive stroke in his brain stem, the nerve center of the body. It was the worst type of stroke. His chance of survival without life support was nonexistent. While he was still physically with us, he was gone.

I hopped on the first flight to Wisconsin. Because of the virus, there was only one. I'd say that I got one of the last seats on the plane, but the truth is there were sixteen people on a flight with about twenty rows and six seats per row. When I arrived at the hospital the next morning, the administrator met us in the lobby and explained that some of the exceptions they made earlier were no longer being offered to us. They were going to let my mom and me in because I had yet to say goodbye. That was it, and only for ten minutes. The hospital was running out of the personal protective equipment required to visit a patient in the ICU, and they had to make some tough decisions regarding future visits until Mike's coronavirus test officially came back. I understood, but that didn't make it any easier.

I tell you all that to set the stage for what happened next. Because as a person with anxiety and OCD who has since battled depression, it stunned me. It foreshadowed more of what was to come.

After we geared up in gloves, gowns, and masks, the nurse ushered me and my mom into the room. As I turned the corner I saw Mike, tubes and wires seemingly coming out of everywhere, his head cocked to the side and slightly bent upward, and his mouth gaping open to accommodate the ventilator. There was a steady, yet eerie, hissing sound of the machine taking his breaths for him. But as I took it all in, I didn't immediately start crying. No disbelief. No tears. No weakness in the knees. Instead, as I stared at the man in front of me, a deep truth I had heard in church all my life surfaced: our bodies are only a part of us, and they are definitely not all of us. Mike's body was just that, his body. What was in front of me was just the shell he inhabited here on earth. And that shell had broken down. Sure, it was a part of Mike, but it wasn't all of Mike. There was so much more to him. And I didn't feel like all of him was there.

To say my mom had a different reaction would be an understatement. She wept the moment we went in. But the weeping quickly gave way to something I will never forget. See, my mom was praying for a miracle. As a nurse, she knew what the medical prognosis was. She knew there was no earthly way Mike was coming back. But she wasn't placing her hope in earthly reports. So, after crying for a bit, she leaned over the rail of the hospital bed and started commanding Mike to wake up. Louder and louder, until she was almost shouting. It went on for nearly the entire time we were in there.

That's when I lost it. *That's* when it started setting in how tough this was going to be. I wasn't crying as much for Mike as I was crying for my mom and what her life was going to be like without Mike in it.

After our ten-minute time limit stretched to about twenty, we were ushered out. Later that day I found myself alone with my mom at my brother's kitchen table. She looked at me, cocked her head to the side, and then asked a pointed question.

"Jonny, are you believing for a miracle with me?"

Before I tell you my answer, I need to tell you this. When I talk about God using our tragedies, our disorders, and our circumstances for our good and His glory, the biggest reason I know that to be true is because of what came out of my mouth next. Because if not for decades of my own internal struggles, if not for the three deaths before this, I would not have been able to answer the way I did.

"Mom, I want so badly for Mike to have a physical miracle. And I am begging God for that. But I am not putting my hope in it. My ultimate view of God, my faith in Him and what I know He can do, is not determined by Mike waking up or not. I want him to, for sure. But I'm more comforted by the fact that God has already done a miracle for Mike. If Mike doesn't wake up, and his physical body dies, we know that's not the end. The ultimate, best miracle has already happened. It's already secured. Better yet, I actually know Mike is going to be healed. What I don't know is if that healing is going to take place on this side of heaven. But the fact is, he is going to wake up. It's just a matter of if he's going to wake up and see us or wake up and see Jesus. I can also tell you that God's at work whether Mike opens his eyes for us or not. I can tell you that God is using and will use Mike for His glory, whether he has a miraculous recovery or not. I just know it. And I have so much confidence in it."

She looked at me with tears in her eyes, then looked to the side and nodded her head as she pursed her lips and took it all in. "Yeah."

I can't tell you where those words came from. But I can tell you they would not have been possible had I never struggled to make sense of not only what has gone on inside of me but also what has gone on around me. Because of my struggles, because of the years of hurt, pain, and wrestling with why I am the way I am and the truths that God helped me see, I was able to convey an understanding of the gospel in a way I have never articulated before and never imagined being able to articulate.

If this book were published any earlier, this chapter would have been only about my sister and one important lesson I learned. Now, through another tragedy and God's faithfulness to use it, it may be the most important thing I've ever written.

As for Mike, fewer than forty-eight hours after I said those words to my mom, on Easter Sunday, his heart stopped beating, his lungs stopped breathing, and his blood stopped flowing. Yet with his physical eyes closed he woke up to see Jesus.

What a miracle.

⌒

Mike was sixty-one years old when he died, nine years shy of the magical seventy-year mark he once said we were all promised. While I don't believe God allowed him to die tragically so that I could make the point I'm about to make, I do believe it's just one of the small ways He's used Mike's death to continue teaching me about Himself.

One thing I've learned over the years is that God often doesn't teach us a lesson just once. Instead, He has to keep revealing the same thing over and over and over again, and like C. S. Lewis said, sometimes that involves shouting to us in our pain.[1] I think that's probably because we have a tendency to forget things easily. The light bulb goes off only to burn out months, weeks, or even days later. My hunch is you have seen this at times in your own life.

A foundational theme over the last two chapters has been that our struggles, whether with mental health or with our loved ones dying, are not punishment for our sins. While there have been several ways the Lord has reminded me of that over the years, His most explicit reminder to me of that truth happened as a result of Mike's death.

Over a decade earlier, Mike told me that dying tragically before your seventieth birthday signaled unrepented sin in your life. That conversation in the car that December day started me on a journey to find out if that was true or not—a journey that showed me that God is not using my anxiety to punish me but rather to refine me. My OCD is not the result of sin in my life but rather of sin in the world that has made this place a far cry from what God originally intended, filled with hardships and struggles. That lesson could not have been made clearer to me than in Mike's death. In many ways, he was Reggie White, the Packers player from the previous chapter who also died unexpectedly. He was kind. He was gentle. He was godly. He was a sinner, yes, but he didn't have some secret, hidden sin. He wasn't being punished. He helped more people in his life than I ever will. He forgave, sometimes to our family's frustration, especially when it involved people taking advantage of him. Mike was one of the most God-fearing men I have ever known. While he had made plenty of mistakes in his life, especially in his younger years as he navigated being a stepdad to four kids, he had become about as close to blameless as I had seen. Yet he's gone. Tragically, suddenly, and unfairly.

I can't say exactly why Mike died, or at least I haven't discovered every explanation, but I can say that God has used his death to solidify everything I discovered as a result of our conversation years earlier. If ever I need a reminder that God is not doling out tragedy and struggle as some sort of cosmic retribution, I look at what happened with Mike. Does that mean I'm completely able to make sense of it? No. That's also a lesson the Lord is continuing to teach me. I need to trust Him even when I can't completely figure out what's going on or why it's happening. That's a lesson you can bet is critical to my mental health as I continue this journey.

I can only imagine what lessons He is teaching you as well.

CHAPTER 4

THE LITTLE WHITE PILL

I REMEMBER FEELING MORE THAN a little overwhelmed in the weeks after my diagnosis. The initial euphoria of naming what was going on inside of me had worn off, and even though I had a foundational understanding of God's goodness and ability to work through my pain, the reality of what was ahead of me started to sink in.

"This is going to be a lot of work," I told myself.

Guess what: it *has* been a lot of work. In those initial weeks and even months it was overwhelming. Why? Because I didn't have a map. I felt like I was dropped into the middle of a forest and told I had to find my way home. Sure, naming what was going on meant I had a compass and a flashlight. But there was still so much unknown.

Where am I?

Where do I go from here?

What direction should I start going?

Is there anyone else around to help me?

What happens if I encounter a river I can't cross?

Eventually, I stumbled and fumbled my way through the woods and found a road. It wasn't easy. I'm not home yet, but I am at least on the right path.

These next three chapters are meant to guide you to that path. I want to save you from as many close encounters, falls, and aimless wanderings as I can. That starts by explaining the approach I have found that has offered me the most relief and the most rest. It's not overly complicated, but that also doesn't mean it's always easy. That approach? It involves taking care of my brain, my body, and my spirit.

Said another way, I have found that treating anxiety and OCD requires a holistic approach. In fact, I have experienced the most rest when I am taking medication (treating my brain), exercising and eating better (treating my body), and pressing into my faith (feeding my spirit). For this chapter, we're going to talk about the brain and medication aspect. But don't be fooled. My medication only puts me in a place mentally to be able to address the other two needs. Yes, they are needs. It's a symbiotic relationship. All three aspects work in harmony with one another.

Think of them as the three legs of a stool that support your mental health:

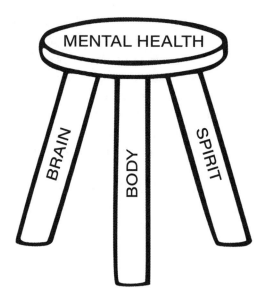

When you look at the diagram, you see that two of those are physical (brain and body) and one of them is spiritual. The key to finding rest amid your anxiety and OCD, then, is recognizing that your mental health is made up of both physical and spiritual components. Your job is to address all aspects. Do that, and you'll be surprised at just how different your life can be. Trust me, I have been.

For now, let's start with the physical, and specifically the brain. To do that, let me tell you a story.

The Phone Call

I vividly remember crying. Not like a child. No, this was much deeper. It came from a place of profound disappointment, hurt, and shame. I sat there in my living room chair and Brett held my head against her chest, telling me it was OK to let it out. Boy, did I ever.

Moments earlier I had had a very tough and very painful conversation. Painful not just because of what was said—although that was a part of it—but painful because of what was *not* said.

It was the spring of 2015 and I was a few months removed from officially being diagnosed with anxiety and OCD. Brett and I had just bought our first house in preparation for our first child and we were settling into what it meant to be homeowners. I learned quickly that as a homeowner there is always something to do, something to fix, something to improve. There's an endless list of projects. That's exactly what I had gotten caught up in. Project after project after project. On this particular night, I realized I had gotten so caught up in the to-do list that I hadn't called home in a while. So I decided to pick up the phone.

But then I hesitated.

There were plenty of things I could fill my parents in on. The house, the pregnancy, work. But there was only one thing I really wanted to say.

That thing was my recent diagnosis and that, at the suggestion of my psychiatrist, I had started taking medication for it. The hesitation was rooted in a fear of how my mom would react to all that. The churches we were brought up in emphasized faith and healing to deal with a lot of your medical issues, especially when it came to mental health. I was about to tell her that I had forgone the faith healing, the forehead anointing, and the "sowing seeds of faith" that were so much a part of my upbringing. I was about to tell her that instead of only relying on prayer, I had opted for a psychiatrist and a counselor and, on top of that, I had decided on treatment that involved medication: a little white pill called Prozac. I knew she wouldn't be ecstatic about any of that.

In fact, I clearly remember a conversation taking place between her and one of my sisters in my teenage years that stuck with me. I can't say for sure the context of the discussion, if it was about my sister or someone else, but I specifically remember it being about treating mental health issues—depression, anxiety, ADD, or something similar—with medication. We had a family business in the health-care field, so conversations like these were normal.* However, what stood out to me was what my mom said about using prescriptions.

"You know, you should avoid getting on psych meds," she said matter-of-factly. "Once you do, you'll always be marked by insurance companies and it will be much harder for you to get coverage in the future."

The point was clear: taking medication for any mental health issue brands you with some sort of scarlet letter you can never get rid of. And after all, instead of turning to meds, you were supposed to turn to your faith anyway. Prayer, faith, and any needed repentance were the key.

On the first part—the one about being branded—she was definitely right. There has been a stigma surrounding mental health; that's a fact. She knew that better than most from her years in the health-care field.

As someone who struggles with OCD and anxiety that can manifest itself in concerns about medical issues, I imagined how awful it would be to not get treatment for cancer because you once took medication for your anxiety. That was scary. Additionally, Mom was the

---

* The four walls of our house heard more conversations about death, Medicare, and referrals than they ever did about, say, sports.

only medical expert I knew. She was not only a nurse but also had taught nursing, and beyond that she owned her own nursing agency. In my world, she was the definitive authority on health care. Who was I to question her? I imagine it would be akin to growing up with your dad as a mechanic. In that scenario, you would take what he said about cars to be the gospel truth. If he told you that having a lot of keys on your key ring would eventually damage your ignition, you would remove the unnecessary keys.* If he told you to never take your car to a dealership to be serviced because they rip you off, you would probably never cross the threshold of Lakewhatever Chevrolet.

As I prepared to make my call, that was all in the back of my mind. While I had obviously developed a different view on the use of medication, I had not encountered anything in the years since overhearing that conversation to indicate that my mom's stance had significantly changed. I was about to find out how right I was.

I dialed my old home phone number by heart and waited for an answer. After a few rings my mom picked up. We exchanged the normal pleasantries, she asked how Brett and the baby were, and then she wanted to know how I was doing. I told her that recently there had been some stuff going on that I wanted to tell her about, stuff that had been difficult and had been causing a lot of issues in my marriage. She gave a slightly drawn-out "Okaaaaay," punctuated with the distinct Midwestern accent that still sneaks its way into my own voice from time to time. I told her about some of my symptoms and that I talked to my sister, Jess, and she recommended I go to a psychiatrist and ask him about anxiety and OCD. I told her I went, and that he had diagnosed me with both.

And then I told her what I feared most. I told her I was taking medication for it.

"Sooooo, yeah. There you have it," I said in the most upbeat way possible, hoping that the peppiness in my voice would coax the reaction I wanted.

---

* My grandpa was a mechanic and once gave this advice to my dad, who gave it to me. I now have the bare minimum number of keys on my key ring.

I waited for a response. And waited. It didn't come. I broke the silence with, "Do you have any thoughts?"

I'll never forget what she said next.

"I don't know, I don't know," she said quickly, as if talking to herself, her voice sprinting out of her mouth. "It just seems like everyone is taking medication for something these days. It seems like everyone has some sort of issue now. Jess says she has the same thing, but I guess . . . I just don't know. I don't know," she repeated in a quick, defeated tone. She paused and then continued, not angrily but in an almost ashamed way, her voice starting to crack. "I just don't know what I did wrong with you kids." And then she went silent.

It stung. I wasn't accusing her of *anything*. My diagnosis had nothing to do with anything *she* did. I was just trying to confide in her. I just wanted to hear that it was OK. I almost broke down right then and there. While she didn't necessarily repeat what she had said about medication from years earlier, she didn't have to. It came out loud and clear. Still, the hurt wasn't about the actual medication. The hurt stemmed from the fact that there was nothing expressed about what I was going through. Nothing about being brave for going to the doctor. No utterances of sympathy or empathy. No trying to understand or talk about wanting me to be better. The strides I had made in the months since naming what was going on retreated with every second of her silence.

I managed to hold it together and decided to end the call as soon as possible.

"Well, I just wanted to give you an update. You should know it's not your fault. Love you."

She told me she loved me too, but once again sounded defeated.

"Talk to you soon . . . OK . . . bye." And with that I hung up and within seconds was being held like a rag doll by Brett.

In that moment, my previous feelings of having power over the diagnosis gave way to shame. Shame that I couldn't do it on my own. Shame that I couldn't muscle through the diagnosis without the medication. Shame that I needed a "crutch." Shame that I was even struggling with these issues in the first place.

In other words, I began questioning what my diagnosis and my treatment said about me. It brought back some of the same fears I had wrestled with in the past.

Is my faith weak?

Why have I disappointed my mom?

Do I need to just stay silent about this?

Is there something I could have done differently?

Why am I like this?

After gathering myself that night, I called my sister Jess to tell her how it went. It was comforting. She explained how she had similar conversations in the past that hadn't gone the best. But she pointed out how much the Word of Faith movement—a movement that emphasized if you had enough faith you could make most health problems disappear—had been a major part of the churches we were raised in and how medication for these types of issues, according to that tradition, was frowned upon.

"Jonny, for them it's all about having enough faith," she reminded me.

As she said that, my mind went back to another conversation I will never forget. I can still picture the hallway where I was when I heard the words. It was one of the churches I had grown up in, with its tired fluorescent lights and that distinct older church smell. I'm sure you've encountered it too. It's the combination of heavy cleaners, a slight mustiness, and years of "pot blessing" scraps being worn down into the stained, brown, leatherlike carpet.

It was a Sunday and I was waiting for my parents to finish socializing after the service when I caught the tail end of a conversation between two of the church's members. They were talking about a young boy who had attended regularly but who had recently died of cancer. The death was devastating for his mother as well as the countless people in the church who had been praying for his recovery. Despite those prayers, despite the commands for the cancer to flee his body, he succumbed to the disease.

"If only his mom had more faith and didn't doubt that he could be healed, he'd still be here," one of them said.

"It makes me wonder if she had unrepented sin," said the other, previewing what my stepdad, Mike, would say years later.

In other words, if only his *mom* had done something different, he might still be with us.

My stomach churned as I remembered those words, and I started shaking my head. It's wrong. It's misguided. It isn't the gospel. Ironically, it's the doctrine of works that so many evangelicals claim to rail against.

I grew silent on the phone. Jess assured me that my mom did, in fact, love me, but that when it comes to mental health issues, she had sat through decades of misguided and incomplete teaching—teaching that sometimes even held the faith of a parent accountable for the struggles of a son or daughter. She reminded me that for decades my mom had a front-row seat in the health-care industry to people being stigmatized because of mental health treatment and it "following them for the rest of their lives."

Jess's words helped put things in perspective. It didn't make all the feelings and questions disappear. That would take time. Still, what it did do was start me on a path to figuring out a proper understanding of the role of medication for mental health issues, especially as it relates to people of faith.

Common Grace

The date was September 3, 1928. A scientist named Alex had just returned to his lab after vacation and was sorting some petri dishes of the staph infection he had been studying. As he moved one, he noticed something odd: mold. Not just any mold. Where the mold had started growing, the staph had retreated. In fact, the mold seemed to secrete some sort of substance that had killed off the staph. It was incredible. It was groundbreaking. And it was an accident.

Alex, by the way, is Alexander Fleming, the modern-day father of antibiotics who discovered penicillin, which was the mold that had formed on his petri dish. Until his accidental discovery, a bad scratch meant you were praying, waiting, and hoping that it didn't lead to a blood infection.* Imagine living like that for a second. But because of a little mold in a petri dish, we no longer fear the deadly implications of a knife slipping and catching our finger while cutting chicken breasts.

The discovery of another drug, Prozac, isn't nearly as interesting. But it's just as important. Prozac is the little white pill I take every day that has helped change my life. Scientists in the late seventies had a theory that regulating the flow of serotonin in the brain could help stabilize people's moods and thus treat depression. They were right. By the fall of 1987, it was approved by the FDA. Then it exploded.

It appeared on the cover of *Newsweek*, which dubbed it "a break-through drug for depression." *Fortune* magazine called it one of the "pharmaceutical products of the century." And by 2002 its sales topped $22 billion worldwide.[1]

Two drugs, two different stories, two world-changing outcomes.

But besides their impact, what do penicillin and Prozac have in common? And why am I going to such lengths to talk about them? Because they both are examples of God's common grace. And common grace is crucial to understanding how and why Christians should consider taking medication for mental health issues.

I'm not sure exactly how old I was when I was first introduced to the idea of common grace, but I think it happened sometime during my college days when I was exploring the book of Job in-depth. The concept became especially real for me, though, after the phone conversation I had with my mom about my diagnosis. It's not a complex, theological idea. In fact, it's all around us and has helped solidify my fundamental understanding of mental health medication.

If you woke up this morning and there was daylight, you experienced common grace. When you taste the richness of a good steak, you experience common grace. When you take antibiotics, antidepressants, or Mucinex, you experience common grace.

---

* I'm summarizing a lot here. Fleming isn't the one who went on to turn penicillin into a medication. That happened over the following fifteen years at Oxford. More here: "Discovery and Development of Penicillin," American Chemical Society, accessed July 2, 2021, https://www.acs.org/content/acs/en/education/whatischemistry/landmarks /flemingpenicillin.html.

God has given all His creatures gifts—gifts that sustain, gifts that heal, and gifts that invoke pleasure, to name a few. He didn't have to make sex enjoyable, art beautiful, or food tasty. He definitely didn't have to make bourbon tasty. But He did. Whether you believe in God or not, whether you consider yourself a Christian or not, the gifts of community, good coffee, and beautiful music continue to surround us. They're gifts given by God irrespective of status, spirituality, or sin. The evil dictator can experience them just as much as the imprisoned believer.

In other words, those things that God has given to all humanity are common graces: the seasons, language, stories, and absolutely the discovery of antibiotics and other medicines.

I revisited the idea of common grace after the conversation with my mom, and as I did the guilt and shame that resurfaced as a result of it began to disappear. I asked myself an important question: *If God has given us these common graces, why would I reject His gift? If He gave us medications to help regulate the chemicals in our brains, why would I categorically dismiss them?*

The stigma continued to fade, and a simple yet profound foundational truth began to form. Just as we wouldn't refuse to see a doctor when a car accident leaves us with a protruding leg fracture, we shouldn't refuse to take medication for serious mental health issues such as anxiety or OCD. Both are foolish choices.

We—those who have struggled with mental health in the church—don't second-guess taking antibiotics for strep throat, but for some reason we were taught to think extra hard about taking medication for our minds. We don't think twice about taking pain medication for a broken ankle, but we hesitate to take it for a broken brain. We take Tylenol for a head*ache*, but we second-guess taking medication for a head *issue*.

Listen, I'm not claiming my view of medicine as a common grace is something that has never been discovered before. In fact, as I continued digging I was relieved to find that this wasn't anything groundbreaking, that what I was uncovering was accepted by reasonable and respectable people, and most importantly that it was biblical. But for some reason it has been slow to take root. It hasn't permeated the church and Christian circles in a way that has made it the default logic. But it's there. And it's important.

"That we have medicine to help us heal physically and psychologically is a gift from Jesus, just as salvation from sins is a gift from Jesus," author Jared C. Wilson explains beautifully.[2]

In fact, did you know Paul recommended taking medication? He did. A few years ago Brett and I were taking a discipleship class at our church and were assigned a tiny book called *Grow in Grace* by a Scottish theologian named Sinclair Ferguson. Near the end he points out 1 Timothy 5:23. I can tell you that I never really paid attention to 1 Timothy 5:23. When you read it in the English Standard Version, it's literally an aside, a parenthetical phrase from Paul to Timothy. It comes out of nowhere. Here's what it says: "(No longer drink only water, but use a little wine for the sake of your stomach and your frequent ailments.)"

I don't know about you, but that sounds a lot like Paul was writing Timothy a prescription for his "stomach and . . . frequent ailments," and that prescription wasn't faith or prayer. It was wine. He recommended a physical answer to a physical problem.

You know what else? In something that is ironically fitting, Ferguson goes a step further in suggesting what some of Timothy's ailments might have been. "He would have found the weakening effect of his sickness a great burden; it may also have been a source of great depression."[3] Depression. Timothy may have had depression, a mental illness. And Paul was recommending a common grace—wine—to fix the underlying issues, which could then help his mood.*

If common grace was good enough for Paul and Timothy, it should be good enough for you and me.

---

* I fully admit this is an extrapolation. Because of that I also want to add a word of caution: treating depression or any mental health struggle with alcohol is not wise. In fact, I myself have to be cautious with my use of alcohol so that it doesn't take on the form of self-medication.

But it wasn't just Paul and Timothy who embraced the idea of common grace. Jesus Himself had something to say about it too. No, really. It appears in His Sermon on the Mount, no less.

As He's explaining to His disciples why it's important to love your enemies, He makes this fascinating point about how the Father's love for all His creation can be seen by looking at the common occurrences in nature. The Father, Jesus explains, cares enough about everyone to allow these common graces: "For he makes his sun rise on the evil and on the good, and sends rain on the just and on the unjust" (Matt. 5:45). Did you pick up on the pronoun before "sun" there? I have read that verse a lot in my life, but until I started thinking about common grace, I never noticed it. The sun is "his." He created it. He set it in motion. He allows it. At any moment, He could take it away, and yet He doesn't. At any moment He could stop the rain. Yet He doesn't. He allows all of us—the just and the unjust—to experience both.

After reading that, it all came together. Just like there was nothing I did to cause my anxiety and OCD (and later depression), God was offering me a gift to help with my issues. It was just there, waiting for me to take it. I could ignore it, but I couldn't ignore it out of existence. If I was willing to use it, I could.

Can God supernaturally heal me of my issues? Of course He can. But what if that's not what He wants for me at this time? For us? And what if He's already offered us some relief? What if He's telling us that He's graced us with a reprieve? Would it not be prideful for us to put a restriction on God and say, "No, Lord, You have to heal me and offer me a way out that I see fit—You have to give it to me on my terms, not Your terms"?

I'm reminded of the modern-day parable of the man who prayed to be rescued during a flood. As the waters rose, the man climbed up on his roof and cried out for God to save him. Shortly after, a man in a rowboat came by and told him to hop in.

"No thanks, I'm praying for God to save me," the man replied. "I have faith!"

The waters rose some more, and the man continued praying. A short time later the police came by in a motorboat and an officer told the man to hop in. Still he refused.

"No thanks, I'm praying for God to save me," he said. "I have faith!"

The water got higher and higher, and the man prayed again. A little while later a helicopter flew over the man's house and the pilot sent down a rope and told him to grab on. Once again he refused.

"No thanks, I'm praying for God to save me," the man shouted. "I have faith!"

Eventually, the waters rose too high and the man drowned. When he got to heaven, he asked God, "Why didn't You rescue me from the flood?"

God replied, "I sent you two boats and you refused to get in. I then sent you a helicopter, and you refused to climb aboard. What more did you expect?"

God sent me a lifeboat in the form of a little white pill. I did nothing to deserve it. And yet He sent it. I decided to climb in the lifeboat. And I thank Him for it every day.

Is Prozac a magic pill that gets rid of all my issues and makes my life bliss? Ha! No way. But it has done something important for me. It has lowered my baseline anxiety enough to allow me to address what's going on inside of me and then put in the work necessary to be a healthier, functioning human being. In other words, the medication mitigates the issues going on in my brain to then allow me to do the physical and spiritual work needed to make me whole. If my anxiety is normally at an eight without medication, I've found Prozac brings it down to a four. When I'm at a four, *then* I'm able to take care of myself physically and feed myself spiritually.

As I was getting ready to write this chapter, I talked with some people who I know have experience with anxiety and depression to get their perspective. One of those people, Tim, is working on his PhD, focusing on how childhood trauma impacts pastors who experience anxiety, depression, and suicidal thoughts. He said something I think you need to hear.

"Whether you're on meds or not, you're still going to have to do the work," he said. "The meds aren't going to do anything about what's going on inside your spirit."

Friends, you're going to have to put in the work. There's no way around it. I'm just telling you that before you can start your job you first need to know where to show up and punch in. That's what medication helps me do.

⁓

By the way, Eli Lilly released Prozac, the little white pill, in December 1987. I was born eleven months earlier.

I'm not foolish enough to claim that it was developed just for me, or heartless enough to ignore the countless others who suffered with mental health issues before then. But I am sappy and sentimental enough to wonder if God knew someday I'd be in this very spot, writing about this very thing, and He would reveal that little nugget to me so I could look back and think about how, from the year I was born, God had something in the works to help me with a struggle I would name nearly thirty years later. It makes me smile.

Revisiting My Mom's Reaction

I'd be lying if I said putting the story about my mom's reaction in this chapter didn't give me some anxiety. I want to honor her and respect her. I thought of ways to take it out. But the more I thought about it, and the more I talked to others who have struggled like I have, I knew how important it was. That's because the story of my interaction with my mom is the story of so many of you. I know there are those of you reading this book who have had that exact conversation or some variation of it with your own mom, dad, friend, pastor, or someone else. I need you to know you're not alone.

I also know there are those reading this book who have been my mom in that moment and are learning for the first time what it means to live with anxiety and other mental health issues, and more importantly what it looks like to be supportive. I can honestly and wholeheartedly look back now and thank God for that conversation, even though it was difficult at the time. Just like I talked about in chapter 2, I believe God has used it for my good and His glory.

As a result, I harbor no ill will against my mom. She loves me, and I love her. We have a wonderful, healthy relationship. Things have happened since that day—events, conversations, phone calls—that have shown me that if we had that same talk today, I believe it would be different. She supports me, this book, and is open to why I'm taking medication. But she still believes for, and wants, a miraculous healing for me. She prays fervently for it. I welcome that. I love that. If God answers that prayer, I will celebrate it and thank Him for it. The great irony, though, is that I believe my mom's underlying prayer for God to intervene in this area of my life is being answered, just not in the way she has always expected.

And today, I can even look back and say I understand her reaction in many ways. Remember the story about the church members wondering if the young boy's mom was at fault for his death from cancer? When I told my mom about my diagnosis, I think there was a tinge of that guilt. She felt as if maybe *she* had done something to cause *my* issues.

"I just don't know what I did wrong with you kids" were her exact words.

She felt like she had, in many ways, failed us. I say "us" because not only does my oldest sister struggle with the same thing as me but also my other sister, Jenny, was an addict who had anxiety and ADD, and my oldest brother's family has battled a host of mental health issues, including bipolar disorder. My mom put all that on her shoulders. Now that I'm a father, I get how easy it can be to fall into that thinking, even if it isn't true. When my daughter is distraught, even though I know I may not be directly responsible, I still put some of the weight on myself. You can know you're not responsible and yet feel fully responsible at the same time.

And in the end, multiple things can be true at the same time. It can be true that Mom's reaction could have been better. It can be true that previous teachings and her bad experiences in the health-care field shaped her perspective. It can be true that she loves me. It can be true that she felt guilty. It can be true that I felt shame, that she felt shame as well, and that I was hurt.

If you're reading this, chances are you've found yourself in a similar conversation with someone you love or respect. Or maybe you can see one of those conversations on the horizon. I want to encourage you in two ways. First, have grace. I know that can be tough, especially if hurtful things are said. But I have learned that people rarely change their minds as the result of one conversation, and especially one charged conversation. Just like it has probably taken you some time to fully understand what's going on and how God is at work, it will likely take others in your life some time as well. Much of this is an education process.*

Second, engross yourself in what you know to be true. Marinate in it. Embody it. Live it. The more you embrace and believe truth, the more people take notice and the easier it is to convey it to them. The more confident you are in what we've discussed up until this point, the easier it will be to help others see it as well. Chapter 10 will lay out all the truths from this book, and each one is important for you to understand.

Until then, hear this truth: God has given me—and all of us—the gift of medication, He has provided numerous means for me to be healthy, and He is continuing to use my diagnosis for my good and His glory. It's a diagnosis that I hope He takes away completely one day. A diagnosis that still manifests itself in dark ways. A diagnosis that can, in many ways, be haunting. Through all of that, though, He has been faithful to show me how to fight back on numerous levels. That is why the next chapter is so important.

---

* That's also why I wrote an entire chapter for your friends and family members who are trying to understand (chapter 9).

CHAPTER 5

THE PHYSICAL BATTLE

BRETT, MY WIFE, HAS A hilarious description of my anxiety when we counsel people about it. It comes down to four letters: BM and AM.

Now that you're sufficiently curious, here's what they mean. BM is "before meds" while AM is "after meds."

She'll say things like, "That was Jon BM. It was not fun," or "That's the way Jon handles it now AM." We'll chuckle, others will chuckle, but in those moments before medication it wasn't always that funny.

In those conversations she's also quick to point out something else: while medication certainly helped, it wasn't the *only* thing that helped. Even though I started taking medication to help mitigate the effects of my disorders, there was still something missing. There was—there is—still work that needs to be done beyond just taking medication. And a big component of that work is addressing my physical health. I have found that I am most whole—I have the most power over my condition—when I am paying attention to my body and what it needs.

That became clear to me in the fall of 2017. Brett and I had reached a point in our marriage where we just could not communicate. Seriously. I would say something I thought was benign and she would take it in a way I never intended, or she would say something she thought was harmless and it would set me off or I would stew obsessively on it for days and draw untrue and unhealthy conclusions. We got to a point where we were both at the end of our proverbial ropes. I was taking my medication but it felt helpless. It felt hopeless. My wife's parents led the marriage ministry at their church, and so they recommended a biblically based marriage counselor in the area whom they trusted and thought could offer some solutions.

So on November 14, 2017, we walked nervously into the office of Mike "the marriage counselor." Mike is a middle-aged man with a goatee and stylish glasses. Ironically, his office was steps away from the wedding chapel where we got married. We sat down and must have looked exhausted. I think we even got in a fight on the way there. We immediately opened up about what had been going on, and it was a productive conversation. But it took only minutes for Mike to realize that I struggled with anxiety and that a key part of the problem was that I had not learned proper, everyday coping mechanisms to help address it. On top of that I wasn't taking care of my body.

As we got to the end, he suggested something I didn't see coming. He said that, yes, couples counseling was in order, but it would not be as effective if we didn't do some work on my anxiety first. Need a dose of humility? Just walk into a marriage counseling session where at the end the conclusion is that *you* are the one who needs to come back . . . alone.

So that day we decided to pause our couples counseling and Mike and I would engage in some one-on-one sessions. We started the following week. To this day I consider the advice I received in those individual sessions to be some of the most helpful I have ever received. They were physical, they were biblical, and they were practical.

How practical? Let me give you an example.

During our first one-on-one session, Mike started by asking me to think about something that had been currently giving me anxiety. It was easy, so I did. I almost instantly felt my heart start to race as my fight-or-flight response kicked in. I felt like I was in a pinball machine, or stuck between two magnets where you're being pulled in both directions at the same time. Once I was there, that's when he asked me some simple questions.

"Jon, do you see that picture above my desk of the nature scene?"

"Yes," I said.

"Focus on it for a second and tell me what you see."

I began to describe the scene. The trees. The river. The mountains in the background. The pines. The green and white birch trees and the yellow wildflowers tickling the shoreline.

"Great," he said. "Now transport yourself there. What do you hear?"

I described the rustling leaves, the water running smoothly along the boulders in the middle of the river, and the song of the blue jays, robins, and cardinals. After a few more questions I had painted with my words a description as if I were right there.

"Now, how do you feel?" he asked.

I opened my eyes, furrowed my brow, and told him, "I feel relieved. I feel calm. I feel at ease. I definitely feel less anxious."

"Jon, what you're doing right now is called mindfulness, and it's something you can use at any time to put yourself in the moment, to pause, reflect, and slow down," he explained. "Mindfulness is an important, everyday technique you can use to battle your anxiety."

Mindfulness. While it isn't some sort of voodoo magic, it might as well have been. It's now one of the most helpful, non-medicinal tools in my toolbox during moments of unexpected anxiety. The idea is that when you feel anxiety coming on, you take practical, physical steps to slow yourself down and stop the attack. You look at what's in front of you or around you, and describe it. Be in the moment.

What are you seeing?

What are you hearing?

What are you smelling?

What are you touching?

Answering those questions forces your mind and body to reset. And it's glorious.

Maybe not surprisingly, this is biblical. I think it's part of what Jesus was getting at when He said, "Do not be anxious about tomorrow, for tomorrow will be anxious for itself" (Matt. 6:34). He's telling us to slow down, to think about what's going on today. I don't know about you, but that verse has traditionally been a frustrating one for me. People have used it in a dismissive way, throwing it at me after I've confided in them about being anxious, or even offering it unsolicited when they sense that an anxious episode is occurring. No other help, advice, or attempt to understand except for saying, "Well, Jesus says don't be anxious." Traditionally, then, that verse has done the opposite of making me less anxious because when I hear it, I associate it with being trite and unhelpful. But since my conversation with Mike, when I think about it in terms of mindfulness and consider that, just maybe, Jesus was laying the groundwork for a practical technique I could use centuries later, it gives that verse new meaning and power. It draws me in instead of pushing me away.

Over the years, I've learned that there are more ways to address my body's physical needs than just mindfulness, some of which Mike helped me discover over our numerous one-on-one sessions. In recent years, a term for this kind of attention has become popular. It's *self-care.* You hear it a lot. It's nothing new. However, as the stigma of mental illness has begun to fade, its popularity has increased. And I couldn't be more excited.

So what does self-care look like, especially for the anxiety sufferer? I'm glad you asked. Here are some of the simple and practical steps I take to address my physical needs, or physical steps I take that then affect my mental health. By taking them, I am put in a better position to fight back against my mental disorders. In other words, I am more whole and more in control when I am paying attention to my body and not neglecting it.

Exercise

About ten years ago I lost over forty pounds by running. I hate running. With a passion. It's so . . . boring. But I realized something interesting: it works. And not just for weight loss but for clearing my head. When I run regularly, there is something that happens to me. My outlook changes. My mood changes. My life is better. My thoughts are less jumbled. I can think more clearly. Science supports that. It's proven that running releases chemicals in the brain that boost your mood.[1]

Maybe you can't run, or you've tried it and no matter what you do it's just not doing it for you. I get that. We're all different. However, you need to find some sort of physical activity to engage in because it will help you.

A few years ago, I got tired of running. A shoulder surgery got me out of my routine and I just couldn't get back into it. I tried biking, but God blessed me with a backside that makes sitting on a tiny bike seat about as appealing as sitting on a pile of fire ants. But I love sports, and I love competition. So instead of running or biking, I started playing racquetball. It was great. My friend Bryan and I would wake up at five in the morning two to three times a week, meet at the gym, and hammer the cover off that little blue ball for an hour. It was fun, it was challenging, and it helped clear my head.

"Lacing up your sneakers and getting out and moving may be the single best nonmedical solution we have for preventing and treating anxiety," writes Dr. John J. Ratey for Harvard Medical School.[2] "As a psychiatrist who studies the effects of exercise on the brain, I've not only seen the science, I've witnessed firsthand how physical activity affects my patients." Exercise decreases muscle tension, changes your brain chemistry, and even activates a different part of your brain that helps with your fight-or-flight response.

The point is clear. Exercise is an important aspect of treating anxiety holistically. When I exercise, it's much harder for my mind to get caught in the endless obsessive cycles. It also provides an outlet for those times when my heart is racing and it seems like I'm on an IV of adrenaline. I've found a direct correlation between how much I exercise and my anxiety. The more I have of the former, the less I have of the latter.

Get Some Fresh Air and Sunshine

As I'm writing this, I'm sitting on a porch overlooking a lake. The sun is shining, and the temperature is perfect. My outlook is glorious and my mind isn't racing. The more fresh air and sun, the better the chances that I'm in a better mood. Ever wonder why you seem to have a better attitude (in general) in the summer? Well, it's science, really: the sun improves our disposition.[3]

"The strongest support for the role of sunlight in health, however, comes from its effect on mood," writes Alice Park for *Time*.[4] In short, the brain produces more serotonin when you get more sun. The more the better, while "lower levels [of serotonin] link to . . . anxiety." That's also the reason depression is more rampant in the winter, when it's darker, and in climates where sunshine is more scarce, such as the Pacific Northwest. So when you have an opportunity to take advantage of the sunshine and its benefits, it behooves you to do so. Even a handful of minutes a few times a week is enough to start experiencing some of the sun's positive effects on your mood.

Eat Better

I said earlier that I lost over forty pounds when I went running. Well, that's not all I did. The other part involved changing my diet. I counted, religiously, my caloric intake. That meant I wasn't "wasting" them on junk like chips and sweets. That's not to say I never ate a Pringle or a Skittle, but you can bet they were treats and not staples. I ate more chicken and fewer burgers. I paid attention to portions. I ate fruit to regularly satisfy my sweet tooth instead of candy. An avocado as a snack instead of a bag of chips is not only better for you but it's also more filling. Here's what I found: when healthy foods are a more intrinsic part of my diet, I feel less anxious, less depressed, and more satisfied. It's just true. In fact, the connection is so important that there's an entire field of medicine dedicated to studying it, and it's called nutritional psychiatry.[5]

Did you know that people who suffer from anxiety should limit their caffeine intake? It's true. "Overall, caffeine is often bad news for people with anxiety," says Susan Bowling, a psychologist at the Cleveland Clinic.[6] It's a stimulant, and it mimics what our bodies naturally do when they're going through an anxious episode, putting us even more on edge. Mix that with an already higher level of anxiety and you have a bad combination.

Additionally, did you know that magnesium and zinc are important minerals in combating anxiety? Or that dietary fiber is key in regulating your blood sugar, and that wild swings in blood sugar levels increase anxiety symptoms? That's true too, and it's important for you to understand.[7] I'm not saying you have to go vegan or paleo or start doing Whole30 365 days a year. Try making some changes for two weeks—start with less caffeine and more fresh foods—and see what it does. At minimum it can't hurt, right?

Find Community

Remember that part in Genesis when God said it was not good for man to be alone? You know what that means, right? We were made for community. We were made to interact. There may be some who read this and dismiss it: "I'm an introvert, so this doesn't apply to me." Wrong. This isn't about being an introvert or an extrovert. This is about engaging in a basic human need.

During the spring of 2020 while self-quarantining because of COVID-19, something odd began happening to Brett, who's an introvert's introvert. She began craving interaction. Yearning for it. Shedding tears over it. Yes, she prefers to be alone, she recoils at the thought of large gatherings, and she'd rather be at a park by herself than at a party. But not seeing people, not hanging out with friends, not being able to go to church—those things all began taking their toll. It became obvious to her: she needed community.

You and I need community too. We need people around us speaking into our lives, challenging the lies that our disorder tells us, and in some cases just helping us get our minds off ourselves and whatever our minds are obsessing over. Is it any wonder, then, why the author of Hebrews says as much? "And let us consider how to stir up one another to love and good works, not neglecting to meet together, as is the habit of some, but encouraging one another, and all the more as you see the Day drawing near" (10:24–25).

I specifically put the idea of community in a chapter about the physical battle because being in community involves a conscious decision to be in proximity with others. You have to "do" community. We all learned many things during the COVID-19 era, and one of them was that no matter how many times you interact with people online (like Zoom), it can never adequately replace the benefits of being in physical proximity.

"Community is critical for us to thrive, especially for someone with mental illness who is already experiencing the common symptoms of loneliness and isolation," writes Stephanie Gilbert for the National Alliance on Mental Illness.[8] In fact, studies have shown that having a healthy friend network reduces stress, especially when contact with that network is face-to-face.[9]

That's no surprise considering how we were created. The truth is you are made for community, and in community you experience a glimpse of the fullness of who God is since He Himself exists in eternal community. Think about that. Not only is community at the beginning of our creation story, but it's also baked into the DNA of who God is. He exists in three persons, Father, Son, and Holy Spirit. So maybe it's no wonder that we are more fulfilled when we are around others as well.

"You cannot be a Christian in isolation; you cannot grow by shutting yourself off from contact with fellow disciples; you cannot adequately receive the help God intends to give you, or properly share the love of Christ," writes Sinclair Ferguson.[10]

That's a strong and somewhat jarring statement. But it's true.

Find community.

Get Away

It might seem odd that I'm following up a charge to find community with advice to get away. The truth is we need to do both.

If Brett is an introvert's introvert, you could call me an extrovert's extrovert. In fact, our marriage almost never happened because of it. The first time we met was at a mixer during college. I was bounding around the room like a politician after a town hall, shaking hands and chatting it up with whoever would listen. Apparently, during one of my stops around the room I met Brett and we started talking. The conversation only lasted a short time because I abruptly ended it and moved on in an effort to try to talk to everyone. She left thinking I was an inconsiderate jerk. It probably helps her case that to this day I don't remember any of that.

I tell you that because as someone who is consistently considered an extrovert, something has happened to me over the last five years that I never saw coming. I have come to not only appreciate but also crave solitude. And as I've cultivated that desire, I have found more consistent relief from my disorders. Don't get me wrong, I still love a good lawn party with cornhole, drinks, and *lots* of people. But in solitude I have begun to find a peace, a rest, and a rejuvenation that I have not experienced before. Science agrees.

"Studies show the ability to tolerate alone time has been linked to increased happiness, better life satisfaction, and improved stress management," Amy Morin writes in *Forbes*. "People who enjoy alone time experience less depression."[11]

Let me draw an important distinction here, though. There's a difference between solitude and isolation. Isolation is retreat. It's not an effort to confront your mental health struggles or combat them; it's running away from them, and it's unhealthy. In solitude, hard work can still get done. In isolation, those issues fester.

Maybe Nathan Foster—son of *the* Richard Foster, who quite literally wrote the book on spiritual disciplines—and his eloquent explanation on the importance of solitude will help you understand:

> In our day God is using the spiritual discipline of solitude as the great liberator. Solitude liberates us from all the inane chatter that is so characteristic of modern life. It liberates us from the ever-present demands that are put upon us; demands

that in the moment feel so urgent and pressing but that in reality have no lasting significance. In solitude the useless trivialities of life begin to drop away. We are set free from the many "false selves" we have built up in order to cope with the expectations others place upon us—and we place upon ourselves. Solitude empowers us to walk away from all human pretense and manipulation.[12]

Do you notice what's prevalent in Foster's description? Contentment. Fulfillment. Solitude involves peace. Isolation, however, involves loneliness and, ironically, can still be quite chaotic. In solitude, you can find God. In isolation, you plummet deeper into your empty self.

Ferguson touches on this. And even though he uses the more general term "isolation" that many are used to, in context he's really talking about solitude: "God wants to teach us lessons in isolation which he does not teach us, or which we cannot learn, in fellowship."[13] That's not always easy, because for someone with anxiety and OCD, to be alone with their thoughts can be scary. But sometimes we need to press into the scary. We need to be scared so we throw ourselves into the arms of the only One who can sufficiently comfort us. It takes practice, especially for someone whose mind races a lot and tends to look for quick fixes. But it's worth it. In an era when technology makes us more available and plugged in than ever, we need to make conscious efforts to unplug, to get away, and to just be.

Sleep

I'm an eight-hours-of-sleep-a-night guy. That doesn't mean I always get eight hours, but I need that in order to feel rested, refreshed, and ready to tackle the day's challenges. Not surprisingly, increased sleep recharges you mentally. When you get more (and better) sleep, you are much better off. Less sleep does the opposite.

"Research . . . found that brain activity after periods of sleep deprivation mirrors brain activity indicative of anxiety disorders," David DiSalvo explains for PsychologyToday.com. "The amygdala—the seat of the brain's fight or flight response—is particularly 'aroused' when we haven't slept enough."[14]

By the way, "deprivation" in this sense doesn't mean staying up for days on end. It can literally be small changes that add up over time that make a big difference. Getting just one night of good, restful sleep can get your mind and body right again.

In the end, Anxiety.org spells it out pretty clearly: "Studies have shown that almost every system of the body is affected by the quality and quantity of sleep a person gets, especially the brain."[15] If you find yourself stuck in a valley, think back to how your sleep has been. Have you been getting enough (generally seven to eight hours a night)? If the answer is no, commit to resetting your sleep habits for a few days and you may be surprised at what it does for your mental health.

That said, let me add an important caveat. Depression sometimes lays us up in bed *too* much and for too long. There is a point of diminishing returns, when added sleep really becomes isolation and does you harm. You have to find the right balance. Be smart enough to know when you're experiencing a depressive episode and need to get your butt out of bed instead of into it.

Serve

I'm going to say something here that at first might sound surprising: anxiety and depression are inherently selfish. That doesn't mean you're selfish for *experiencing* them, or that you're selfish for talking about them. Not at all. What I mean is that they are inherently self-focused. You are constantly thinking about how this or that will affect *you*. You're constantly thinking about how *you* feel and how *you* want to feel better. Sound familiar? Think back to the discussion on isolation. When you're isolating, you're thinking mainly about yourself. It's important to break that cycle, and to do that you need to take the focus off yourself.

Sometimes the best self-care involves caring for others. And once again science backs this up, showing that selflessness and service affect both our minds and our bodies.

"Studies have found that helping others has tangible benefits, both mental and physical, from lowering your blood pressure to reducing feelings of depression," writes Kayleigh Rogers, who herself struggles with anxiety. "And research hasn't found any significant difference in the types of volunteering—any kind of helpful act can create benefits."[16]

She goes a step further and offers a personal anecdote: "When I finish a volunteering session, my muscles are more relaxed, as is my breathing. My mind is also not whirring with worry the way it usually does, and I feel energized to take on the rest of the day."

When you start looking outside yourself, when you turn your gaze elsewhere, it does something to you. Feel yourself in a destructive cycle? Can't get out of a funk? Think about doing something for someone else. Make a meal. Make a call (that's not about you). Volunteer your time. I'm telling you, it helps.

Take a Shower

Yes, I'm telling you to take a shower. Maybe you need the reminder right now. But the larger point is this: invest in your hygiene. Make yourself feel clean. Make yourself feel pretty. Take care of your body. Once again, during the self-quarantine part of COVID-19, the days started blending together. Was it Monday? Friday? Wednesturday? The clothes I was wearing all started to look alike, probably because they were and I wasn't changing them as often. I started losing my hair right after college, so since then I've been shaving my head. During COVID-19, it was getting pretty "long" in my terms. I've had a beard since high school and it was becoming quite bushy and unkempt.* I started finding myself anxious and even teetering on depressed. I took a look at myself in the mirror and knew what I had to do. I had to clean up. So I did. I took a long shower. I trimmed my beard and

---

* In fact, I've started to get gray hairs in my beard. One evening, my daughter was sitting on my lap, looked up at me, and started bawling. I mean, full-on tears. I asked her what was wrong. Her response? "Daddy, you're getting gray hairs and that means you're turning into a grandpa. I don't want you to be a grandpa. I just want you to be my daddy." Heart melted!

shaved my head. I used my semi-expensive aftershave balm. I dabbed on the beard oil. And I felt better. I invested in myself, and it lifted my spirits.

So one of the tangible practices I put in place for the rest of home confinement was making sure I showered every morning, no matter what, and shaved my head. I even bought a somewhat expensive electric razor specifically for bald heads. It was worth it. There's something about cleaning your body that refreshes your mind. The physical water washes over your body, while the figurative water washes over your mind. It gives you a different outlook, one that says you're ready to tackle the challenges of the day, that you're worth it, and that you're going to make it. Try it and see what you think.

Put Your Phone Down

They say you preach against your worst sin. This is me doing just that. When my daughter, Annie, was four, she started playing this little game, except we had no idea she was playing it. We would be at home getting ready to leave, or wanting to make a call, and our phones would be nowhere to be found. Gone. Missing. We'd ping them, but we couldn't hear them. The first time it happened, a frustrated Brett called out to Annie, asking her if she knew where our phones were. With a sly, small smile on her face, she ran to her playroom and dug them out of God knows where and brought them to us. We asked her why she did it, and the answer made us want to collapse: "I wanted you to stop looking at them so much." Talk about a knife to the chest. Soon after that we bought a timed lockbox where we would put our phones in "time-out" during family time.

The truth is our screens have consumed us. I can't tell you how many times I've found myself mindlessly scrolling through Facebook or Instagram, only to find that sometimes hours have gone by. With that has come scientific proof of increased anxiety and depression, especially in young people.[17] You can do a simple Google search and find that excessive screen time is linked to everything from neck pain to worse sleep. Social media leads to unhealthy bodies, unhealthy lifestyles, unhealthy comparisons, unhealthy expectations, and unhealthy relationships. Want to hit the reset button? Try setting limits on your screen time and see what happens. Or just get your four-year-old to hide your phone.

⌒

I hope these suggestions are helpful for you. They've been helpful for me. And I know they've been helpful for others. With that said, I need to admit something: while these last two chapters have focused on medical and physical ways to overcome your mental health disorders, my fear is that you would get to this point and ignore everything I'm about to say going forward, that you'd think the pages up to this point have all the answers. They don't. In fact, what I'm about to cover is the most crucial aspect of battling your anxiety and investing in your mental health. To ignore what I'm about to say would be like driving your car on only two wheels. Can you do it? Yeah. Are you limiting yourself? Absolutely. Is it wise? No. And in the end, why would you want to?

Anxiety and OCD are not merely physical issues with physical solutions. There's something else at play. Something bigger. Something deeper. That something is spiritual. You can't read this chapter or the previous one without the next one and expect to find rest. You just can't. So please, for your sake, don't stop here.

CHAPTER 6

THE SPIRITUAL BATTLE

IN ORDER FOR ME TO be able to put these words to paper, Brett sacrificed a lot. One of those sacrifices looked like regularly sending me away to my in-laws' lake house, always for one weekend a month, Friday through Sunday, and twice for a week at a time. The goal was to be alone and focused. No work, no kids, no responsibilities, no distractions. She would take the kids, with no complaints, and make sure I was in the best environment to succeed. You would not be reading this right now if she didn't love me in that way.

On those weekends, I packed my overnight bag with the bare essentials, such as sleeping shorts, some underwear, toiletries, food, a little bourbon, and my running clothes and shoes. Everything I'd need for a productive weekend.

One particular weekend, though, I messed up. I was in a hurry to get out of town before traffic got bad, and I quickly threw my bag together at the last minute, kissed Brett and the kids goodbye, and hit the road. I got caught in traffic anyway and ended up arriving at the house late. I ate a little something and went to bed, hoping to wake up refreshed and ready to write in the morning. And for the most part, that's what happened.

But I'm a morning person. What that means is that until about two in the afternoon, writing comes fairly easily. The words flow, the ideas just seem to click, and I can sometimes have thousands of words completed before I even break for lunch. The afternoon? That's a different story. Things slow down significantly. I catch myself staring off into space searching for the right phrase or idea. My eyes start getting heavy and my brain feels like quicksand. It's at that time that I usually head to my overnight bag, grab my running clothes and shoes, and hit the pavement. It clears my head, wakes me up, and rejuvenates me for the next round of writing.

On this particular day, that's what I went to do. The ferocity of the keyboard clicking had gone from sounding like chipmunk chatter to a five-year-old finger-pecking on a typewriter. So I headed down to change. When I went to unpack my bag, there was something missing: my running shoes. I had my hat, my shirt, my shorts, even my phone holder. But no shoes. And I don't know if you've ever tried to run a few miles in Crocs, but it isn't pretty. Needless to say, I didn't go running.

Why do I tell you that? Because addressing your anxiety without dealing with what's going on spiritually is like trying to go on a run without your shoes. You can have the right intentions, the right clothes, and the right equipment, but if you don't have shoes, you're not going anywhere.

Similarly, you could be faithfully taking your medication, you could have your nutrition dialed in, but if you're not feeding your spirit—if you're not investing in your relationship with Jesus—you're never going to experience true, sustained rest. Can you run without shoes? You *can*. But you're not going to get far. Can you experience moments of rest or relief if you neglect your relationship with Christ? You *can*, but it's not going to last long, and it's certainly never going to be as fulfilling as when you invest in that relationship.

To ignore the spiritual aspect of battling mental health issues is as much a misguided approach as it would be to dismiss the value of medication. We are spiritual beings. Mental health issues are not *only* spiritual issues with spiritual answers, but they are certainly not devoid of them.

I said earlier that I am at my best when I am attacking my anxiety and OCD in a threefold way: brain, body, and spirit. Remember the stool diagram from chapter 4? Two of the legs supporting our mental health are physical (brain and body). The third leg is spiritual. If you get rid of the spiritual leg, the stool (our mental health) is still unstable, no matter how strong the other two are. Your battle against anxiety, OCD, and other mental health issues is too important *not* to be feeding your spirit regularly.

Which One Is More Important?

The natural questions I'm sure you're asking (because I've asked them myself) are: "So which aspect is more important, the physical (brain and body) or the spiritual? Where do I start? What deserves more attention?" Those are not bad questions, but I think they are the wrong ones.

The better question is: where am I currently most deficient?

The man who runs four miles every morning, eats only the cleanest foods, takes his medication religiously (if he's on it), practices mindfulness, and sleeps eight hours a night but still finds himself struggling needs to examine his spiritual life.

The woman who gets up early, reads her Bible, is engaging in Christian community, and listens to sermon podcasts on the way to work but still finds herself struggling needs to examine her physical life.

To be fair, let me say I've never found figuring out where I'm most deficient to be that clear or simple in my own life. I don't expect it to be in yours. The truth is it's almost always a combination of both the physical and the spiritual. But there will be times when the deficient aspect comes running out of the house yelling, screaming, and firing off a shotgun like a Kentucky moonshiner to get your attention. That day in the coffee shop when my hatred of Splenda was put on full display—the turning point years ago when I realized that I needed to seek help—was the physical wake-up call for me.

I can't say I've had a spiritual wake-up call in that same way. At least nothing that dramatic. Instead, the reminders of my spiritual deficiencies come in moments when I feel like I'm in a desert. When I'm doing "everything right," or so I have convinced myself, and still feel stuck in a rut. It comes when I catch myself relying on what I think I can do more than what I know God can do and end up burning out. It comes when I catch myself looking for something to worry about. It comes when I'm being short with Brett about trivial things. It comes when I have to think hard about the last time I spent any meaningful time in prayer.*

But while the physical and spiritual can trade off with which one needs more of your attention, I don't think you can ever fully understand the physical until you understand the spiritual. In other words, we can only understand ourselves better when we understand God better. I can tell you unequivocally that I only fully grasped the truths in this book once I began understanding the truths about the One who created them, who created me.

In that sense, then, while the last chapters were about the physical, it's the spiritual that forms the foundation by which everything else makes sense.

As I have thought about, experienced, and sought to understand the interplay of the physical and the spiritual in battling anxiety, Paul Miller has been one of the most helpful guides in understanding how the two are connected. In *A Praying Life*, he explains it perfectly: "While antidepressants and counseling have helped many people, including me, the search for a 'happy pill' or 'happy thoughts' will not stop our restless anxiety. It runs too deep."[1]

How true. Our anxiety, our OCD, our depression are like thorny bushes. It's easy to see their effects above the surface, but we will never get rid of them by simply trimming the branches. Their roots penetrate into the depths of our souls.

---

* I'm not talking about prayer for my disorders here specifically. I'm talking about prayer in general. As I'll explain later, what I've come to understand about prayer and what it does for our relationship with God is significant.

However, there's something important you need to understand. I briefly mentioned it in chapter 4 but I want to reiterate it and unpack it here. I've learned that because of some of the physical deficiencies in my brain, it becomes nearly impossible to focus on the spiritual aspect unless I'm taking my medication. In other words, my medication makes it so that I am able to dig into the important spiritual truths. My medication acts as a trimmer, cutting down the overgrowth so that I can get to and address the roots. The physical tips we talked about in the previous chapter help with that as well, which is why I specifically chose to place that chapter ahead of this one.

Recently, Brett and I became aware of a friend who had a severe eating disorder, to the point where she was only consuming about a thousand calories per week. It had gotten so bad we begged her to check into a facility, but she refused. Because she was an adult, there was not much we could do. Still, we kept pushing her. Finally, after numerous conversations and a lot of prayer, she agreed to at least go see a counselor who specializes in eating disorders. But after only a few sessions the counselor told her it was pointless. Why? Because this young woman was so physically deficient—her body was so starved for food—that the counselor couldn't even have productive conversations about the underlying issues that were, ironically, feeding the disorder. The counselor could never help her address the roots until she confronted her immediate, physical needs.

For me, addressing my disorder in a physical way (medication plus what I mentioned in the previous chapter) puts me in a position where I am able to address, face, and attack the roots of what is going on within me. It gives me the best chance to address the deeper spiritual issues, which feed what's going on in my brain.

The Spiritual Issues

So what exactly are those deeper spiritual issues that I—that we—need to address? God is revealing them to me regularly, which is the beauty of drawing closer to Him. By the way, I have learned to welcome and not fear those revelations. But isn't that kind of the opposite of what we have been taught to do? How many times have you heard, "Don't pray for humility, because God just might answer your prayer by humbling you"? I get so confused and frustrated by that. Isn't that the point?

If God has revealed pride to be an issue in your life and it's wreaking havoc on your work, ruining your relationships, and alienating your family, don't you *want* Him to answer your prayer for humility? If we truly see something as a problem, then why would we prioritize the temporary pain over the long-term relief? If you see a friend with a nail through his thumb, you would never tell him, "Be careful about going to the doctor and asking him to remove it, because he just might pull it out, and that can hurt." Of course there's going to be some pain before, during, and after he removes what's not supposed to be there.

We would never advise people to sacrifice their overall health because getting better could be a little painful. Yet so many times we tell people to sacrifice their spiritual health because the sanctification process can get uncomfortable. Stop it!

That leads me to the four spiritual issues God has shown me are at the heart of my anxiety. I also think they're at the heart of yours. They're the issues we need to work on rooting out, because they're like a cancer that's slowly eating us alive—they start in the heart and then move to the mind, and before we know it they have buried us in a coffin of lies.

1. We struggle to believe that God has everything under control.

We may say we believe God is all-powerful and all-knowing, but then we don't act like it. I remember in 2014, my Green Bay Packers ("we") started off 1–2. This was just a few years after winning the Super Bowl, so expectations were still high. Quickly, fans started panicking: "What's wrong with the team? Are they declining? What are they going to do? Is the season lost?" In response the team's quarterback, Aaron Rodgers, famously went on the radio and told everyone to "R-E-L-A-X." They went on to finish 12–4 and came within an overtime loss of returning to the Super Bowl.

So what's my point? We can sometimes—many times—play the role of impatient sports fans when it comes to God. When things aren't going quite how we think they should go, we doubt His ability and start asking all sorts of questions. "What's wrong? Where's God? Why haven't I gotten a response? What will others think about me? What's *He* thinking about me? What if the worst-case scenario I'm thinking in my head right now comes true? How will I ever financially recover from this?" My hunch is you read those questions and were able to relate. That's because, like Thomas, we anxious people tend to default to doubt.

2. We struggle to believe that God loves us.

We talk a lot in our churches about the intimate love of God, and yet how many times do we act like He's disinterested in what's going on in and around us? The answer for me is "a lot." I bet it's the same for you.

I recently completed a nine-month discipleship program at my church. You know what we focused on the entire time? One simple truth: God loves us and thus cares deeply about us. The idea is that if we live like we believe He loves us, our lives would be radically different. It's true. So many of my own sin struggles can be traced back to either not really believing God loves me and cares about me or at least not internalizing it.

If you truly believe the God who created the universe loves you, would you go searching for fulfillment in so many other things? Would you doubt Him? Would you not trust that what He says about Himself and about you are true? Would you not believe that He's working this struggle for your good?

Instead, though, I often catch myself treating God like an eternal toy maker who wound me up, set me down, and just let me go. He's not *really* concerned about me. I view Him as hands-off and convince myself He has many more important things to worry about than my silly day-to-day issues. You know what? That view creates a gap between Him and me, and into that gap pours all sorts of lies that push me further and further away from Him. The further I am from Him, the closer I am to something else, and "something else" looks like a myriad of other God "substitutes" that can never fulfill my spiritual longings. They certainly can't bring me the rest I'm truly seeking.

3. We want to be God and control everything around us.

The previous two struggles lead us to this one. When we either doubt God's abilities or doubt His love for us, we then feel a need to step in, to take control, to try to fix things and make them go our way. Rarely does that work out.

I seem to default to this often when I'm forced to wait. For example, when I find myself in the aftermath of a less-than-ideal interaction with someone, I'm prone to overdoing it. What I mean is that I'm often quick to send a text or shoot an email to try to make comfortable any uncomfortable situation. When I don't get a response in what I deem is an appropriate amount of time—and instead of trusting that the Lord is in control—I send another. And another. And another. And almost every time I either say something I shouldn't or I exacerbate the issue, leading to more frustration and worry. If in those situations I would take a step back and let God be God and do what God does, I could find the peace I so desperately crave. But so many times I let my mind's unease cloud His truth.

If you're married (or in a relationship), you've seen this play out firsthand too. How many times have you asked your spouse to do something, only to do it yourself out of frustration when they didn't do it how or when you wanted them to? And how many times did that end up going well for you? Maybe you rushed it, or your frustration led to hurt feelings, or you failed to take into account why they were doing it differently, only to learn that their way was, in fact, better. We treat God like that a lot. At the first sign of discomfort or frustration, we turn inward and act as if He needs our help on this one. Unfortunately, though, we *always* overestimate our ability to control situations, circumstances, and people. We can't see everything at play like God does. We see one scenario, He sees infinite ones. We contemplate a few outcomes, He sees them all. We're looking out for one person, while He's "got the whole world in His hands."*

4. We have a tendency to turn to things other than God in order to find relief.

When we step in and try to take control, not surprisingly we get overwhelmed. That, in turn, leads to more anxiety. It's a vicious cycle. Since our gazes are turned inward, we frantically look for things to give us instant relief. Sound familiar?

Historically, for me, those cheap reliefs have been everything from alcohol and porn to food and social media—anything that can distract and offer a temporary reprieve from the feelings of helplessness or hopelessness, and especially the racing thoughts. You know what that's called? Self-medicating. It's why so many people with mental health issues struggle with addiction.† It's why I need to be mindful of my alcohol intake, especially during bouts of anxiety, so I don't use it to numb, hide, or distract myself from my feelings. It's why I also need to be careful that when rampant, overzealous thoughts consume me, I don't turn to the Chinese buffet. That may sound oddly specific and a little funny, but the truth is that I have a tendency to gorge myself on cheap Chinese food (especially those glorious crab rangoons) as a way to bury my feelings when I find myself in difficult situations. But sesame chicken, as well as those other substitutes, not surprisingly, never lead to the fulfillment I'm looking for. They never give the long-lasting relief I'm craving. Instead, they lead to emptiness and, many times, regret.

A Pride Issue

You know what all four of the struggles just mentioned have in common? It's something that you see peeking through especially in number

---

* A little cheesy? You bet. But I just couldn't resist! (Now enjoy having that song stuck in your head if you know it.)
† I've since come to understand that my youngest sister's drug addiction was her self-medicating for a slew of mental health issues. One of my biggest regrets is that I didn't understand some of these truths sooner so that I could empathize with her and ultimately be in a better position to help her.

three. It was profound for me when I made the connection. In the end, the spiritual problem at the heart of many of my mental health struggles can be summed up in one phrase: I have a pride issue. You have a pride issue.

My anxiety and OCD lie to me constantly about a lot of things. There is one lie that is foundational to all the other lies, and that's that I am more capable, more reliable, and more trustworthy than God. That lie convinces me that I can step in and make things better, and that I can figure everything out and make sense of it all if I just try hard enough. It says there are things better than God that can help me, and it says my feelings are paramount to the truths He's laid out. That shouldn't be surprising because it's the first lie we ever believed. It's the lie the serpent told in the garden: we can be like God (Gen. 3:1–7).

That foundational lie makes it hard for us to trust that God is in control and will work all things for our ultimate good and His ultimate glory. That poses a big problem, because the truth that He *is* working is at the heart of finding rest. But instead of turning to God and trusting in Him, we turn to ourselves and try to play Him. Again, Paul Miller has been helpful:

> Anxiety wants to be God but lacks God's wisdom, power, or knowledge. A godlike stance without the godlike character and ability is pure tension. Because anxiety is self on its own, it tries to get control. It is unable to relax in the face of chaos. Once one problem is solved, the next in line steps up. The new one looms so large, we forget the last deliverance. . . . We become anxious when we take a godlike stance, occupying ourselves with things too great for us. We return to sanity by becoming like little children, resting on our mothers.[2]

That last line is the key. The spiritual prescription for fighting our pride is admitting and accepting our weaknesses like a child and resting in what we know to be true of the Lord. What is true? It's the opposite of everything above.

- God *does* have everything under control.
- God *does* care about us and have our best interests in mind.
- We make horrible gods and *can't* control everything around us.
- We are most complete when we turn to *Him* for fulfillment.

When we embrace those spiritual realities and let them permeate our souls, we begin to see what it looks like to find some relief. I'll admit, though, embracing those truths is easier said than done. It takes practice. It takes time. It takes discipline. That's where Richard Foster comes in.

Spiritual Disciplines

Earlier in the book I told you that during college I began making my faith my own. I began reading ferociously for the first time in my life. By God's grace, I was surrounded by people who introduced me to some very influential authors, who then introduced me to some of the most influential concepts. One of those authors was Richard Foster. In his masterpiece, *Celebration of Discipline*, Foster taught me how the physical and the spiritual are intrinsically connected. He taught me how practicing certain spiritual disciplines grows us and shapes us by bringing us closer to Christ.* His lessons are ones I continue turning to, and they are fundamental to shaping my battle against my anxiety and finding rest.

In his book, Foster lays out twelve disciplines that enrich our re-lationship with God: meditation, prayer, fasting, study, simplicity, solitude, submission, service, confession, worship, guidance, and cele-bration. It would be futile for me to try to unpack all of them here. (Even if I were to try, Foster does the best job of that in his book, which you should read.) And while I have found all of them to be life-giving, I want to highlight a few that have been especially helpful in building

---

* The very concept of a "spiritual discipline" perfectly illustrates the interconnectedness of the physical and spiritual. You can't practice anything without taking physical ac-tion. You can't study, pray, or meditate without at minimum using your physical mind. It really is a beautiful picture of how God created us.

me up spiritually so I can do battle against my anxiety and OCD. I think they'll help you too. All three of these disciplines, by the way, are part of what Foster calls "the inward disciplines."

1. Meditation

I can't tell you how many times over the years some well-meaning person has told me to "meditate on the things of God" during discussions on anxiety. And I can't tell you how many times I have rolled my eyes. You probably have too. That's because when an anxious person hears, "Just meditate on the things of God," we generally hear something to the effect of, "The answer to your problem is so simple: if you'd just read Scripture more you'd be fine." Listen, I'd love to just be able to open the Bible, pick a Scripture, read it, think about it, and have it bring me peace. But it just doesn't work like that. You know why? Because real, true meditation is much more than that. It's deeper and richer.

That doesn't mean it's more complicated, though. Foster makes that abundantly clear.

Throughout the book he makes an effort to simplify it. "Christian meditation, very simply, is the ability to hear God's voice and obey his word," he writes.[3] That description tears down some of the unhelpful iterations so many of us have heard (like, "Just open the Bible and read") while simultaneously building up a richer, more vibrant picture of what true meditation is and how it can be helpful. What is that picture? It isn't as much about opening a book as it is about opening up your mind to the truths of the Lord—truths He's trying to teach you—and communing with Him. It's about getting to a place and in a posture that allows you to hear God's voice. It involves slowing down, many times finding a space that's physically calming, ridding yourself of distractions, and concentrating on the things of the Lord in a way that gives them the chance to rush over you. I like to think of it as the difference between being stuck out in the sun on a hot day versus sitting in a steam room. Both leave you hot and sweaty, but the latter is more of an intentional, immersive, deliberate experience. By the way, if this sounds familiar you shouldn't be surprised. It's an awful lot like the mindfulness we discussed in the last chapter, but with more of an overt spiritual bent.

I've found some of my best meditation sessions, then, to be when doing yard work, fishing, or taking an extended walk. In those times, I've been able to empty myself of the physical and mental distractions, concentrate on "a single event, or a parable, or a few verses, or even a single word," as Foster suggests,[4] and then let the spiritual truths rush in and take root. It's beautiful. It's life-giving. It's restful.

2. Prayer

Once again, some of the most unhelpful advice I've ever gotten has been, "Just pray about it." Maybe if you're a pastor or a seminarian, that sounds slightly blasphemous. But ask anyone who has struggled with anxiety or other mental health issues and you're going to hear something similar. That's because the problem with that statement is it's often said dismissively as a way to end a discussion instead of press into one. When someone doesn't know what else to say or isn't fully qualified or prepared to offer advice in the midst of a mental health struggle, they tell you to "Just pray about it." When you hear it, then, it feels like being thrown a lifeline that's just a few feet short.

That's probably exacerbated by the fact that we Christians generally struggle with the idea of prayer. For years I know I did. For a long time it felt impersonal and burdensome, like a task I knew I wanted and needed to complete but didn't understand how to or why it was so important.

Doesn't God already know everything I'm thinking, everything I want and need, and how everything is going to turn out? I would ask myself. It constantly hung over my head. That is until I read Paul Miller's *A Praying Life*, and that's when the idea of prayer clicked for me. The biggest takeaway? Prayer isn't at all about prayer.

"Prayer is simply the medium through which we experience and connect to God," Miller explains.[5] He goes on:

> Oddly enough, many people struggle to learn how to pray because they are focusing on praying, not on God. Making

prayer the center is like making conversation the center of a family mealtime. In prayer, focusing on the conversation is like trying to drive while looking at the windshield instead of through it. It freezes us, making us unsure of where to go. Conversation is only the vehicle through which we experience one another. Consequently, prayer is not the center of this book. Getting to know a person, God, is the center.[6]

For much of my life I have treated prayer, or what it can give me, as the end instead of the means. But that couldn't be further from what prayer is meant to be. Prayer is a conversation. It's our primary means through which we cultivate a relationship with the One who can give us rest. It doesn't have to be this stuffy, highly regulated practice that we should fear. Once I realized that it's hard to mess up a conversation between you and God, my prayer life changed. Now, sometimes my prayers are three words repeated over and over again ("Help me, Jesus!"), sometimes they happen while I'm driving, while other times they need to be longer, carved-out sessions where I use prayer cards. As a result, prayer is no longer something I dread or fear I'm doing wrong, and my relationship with God is richer.

That brings me back to the "Just pray about it" advice. In the end, when someone says those words in that context, I can't help but think they are treating prayer as the end in itself: "If you just complete the ritual enough times, you will find the answers you're looking for." But that's not the advice we anxiety sufferers need at all. Remember, we so easily fall into the trap of believing repetition breeds relief. Instead, we need to be led to—and find—what's at the heart of prayer: a relationship. Better advice, then, might be asking the anxiety sufferer, "What has it looked like for you to seek the Lord on this issue, and what do you feel like He's telling you?"

By the way, after reading what Miller says about prayer and finally understanding the heart of what it is and the relief it can bring, I was able to go back to Foster and appreciate something he had told me years earlier in his book: "Real prayer is something we learn."[7] It took me years to understand that. Now, real prayer (prayer that cultivates my relationship with God and brings me closer to Him) has become one of the most enriching and necessary spiritual tools to battling my anxiety.

3. Study

One of the most important things we can do to combat our anxiety is to seek out the truth God has revealed not just to us but to others. While that truth doesn't always take the form of words (Rom. 1:20), many times it does. It's why I have no reservations in pointing you to other, wiser people who have contributed to my own understanding of these issues. Whether that's Richard Foster, Paul Miller, or the apostle Paul, God has used and is using others to convey who He is, what He's done, and what He wants for us. The spiritual discipline of study—the idea that we need to engage our minds in truth—is essential to our spiritual growth and our battle for our mental health.

"Many Christians remain in bondage to fears and anxieties simply because they do not avail themselves of the Discipline of study," Foster writes.[8] Through the study of truth, "ingrained habits of thought are formed."[9] And our thought habits are exactly what need to be rewired. It makes me think of Romans 12:2 and how by renewing our minds we are then able to discern what is "good and acceptable and perfect."

Study and meditation, not surprisingly, play off of each other. Once you have studied something, it's only natural—and necessary—to turn to meditation to let those truths sink even further into your spirit. And once they sink further into your spirit, they take hold and become like strong walls that can help defend you against the lies that your anxiety attacks you with. In fact, by giving truth more real estate in your mind and spirit through study, you leave less room for the lies to build a home.

‿‿

I am most at peace when those three spiritual disciplines are a regular part of my life. I am most at rest when they seep their way into my conversations, my thoughts, my routines, and my actions. Is it easy? Absolutely not. I wouldn't be writing this book if it were. But it is true. My responsibility, then, is to feed my spirit in a way that brings those truths to light as much, and as often, as possible.

But while those are things I've found helpful to practice, there are also things I've learned I need to avoid. I'm potentially stepping into a minefield here, but I'm going to say it anyway because I think it needs to be said. On my list of things to avoid are certain music, movies, and TV shows that not only don't build up my spirit but also can tear it down. It's not that I don't *want* to consume them (my flesh makes sure of that), but I know I *shouldn't*. Let me give you an example. At first glance it may seem controversial. I hope by the end it is not.

The show *Game of Thrones* became one of the most popular shows in history during its run from 2011 to 2019. The writing, the cinematography, and the acting drew acclaim from critics and created a rabid fan base. Its popularity has continued even now that the show has concluded. Brett and I absolutely love dramas like *Game of Thrones*. If there's a movie or show that involves medieval Europe, kings, queens, knights, and battles, we've probably seen it. We can't get enough. So as *Game of Thrones* grew in popularity in the late 2010s, we were convinced it was going to be our new binge show.

Then we saw the statistics.

From seasons one to seven, there were 17 rapes or attempted rapes and 144 instances of on-screen nudity, with 88 percent of them involving women.[10] That's a lot and seems excessive. And that's not just me saying that. In fact, mainstream publications of all stripes took notice, were shocked, and began to speak out. "Frequent and often outlandish, the show's eroticism often overshadows or distracts from the actual story," the *Washington Post* said in 2012.[11] "Why does the show feature so much *sexual violence*—most, though not all, directed at women and even young girls?" the *Atlantic* asked in 2015.[12]

That led Brett and me to an important question: if non-Christians are appalled, shouldn't we as Christians be even more so? That's when we determined, together, that putting that into our heads was not a good idea. Especially my head. I've mentioned that for years I struggled with a porn addiction. That addiction was fueled a lot by my inability, especially before my diagnosis, to "take captive" thoughts that would enter my head (2 Cor. 10:5). It's hard enough for a man who doesn't have OCD to get vivid thoughts and images out of his mind. For me, you can magnify that by ten.

What you watch affects you. In fact, studies have shown that an increase in watching cable TV lowers your IQ.[13] If that's what it can do to your brain, can you imagine what it can do to your spirit? Luckily we don't have to. "Popular television series like *The First 48* and *Scandal* that depict murder, rape, and terrorism are more likely to cause anxiety in viewers," writes Jazmine Polk for Health.com.[14] She found that her favorite show, *Law & Order: Special Victims Unit*, with its graphic "ripped from the headlines" story lines, was giving her anxiety and causing her to lose sleep at night, so she went searching for answers.

"People who are sensitive, emotional, anxious, or depressed are more affected by these shows," Dr. Carole Lieberman, who studies violence in TV programming and the media, told Polk.[15] So what did Polk do? She stopped watching the show.

Sometimes you can experience addition by subtraction.

With all that said, I don't condemn you if you have watched all the seasons of *Game of Thrones*. This isn't a lecture meant to shame you and get you to cancel HBO or chuck your TV out the window. I happen to love movies and television. However, what I am encouraging you to do is to be more selective about what you're watching. I hope you'll realize that what we consume either nourishes us or comes out as waste. The more we're consuming "whatever is true, whatever is honorable, whatever is just, whatever is pure, whatever is lovely, whatever is commendable" (Phil. 4:8), the healthier we are physically, emotionally, and spiritually.

Does that mean I'm only watching reruns of *I Love Lucy* and Charles Spurgeon documentaries? Trust me, if you were to sit across from me at a coffee shop, we could probably talk about shows and movies I have watched in the past that are just as bad as *Game of Thrones*. The point is not to come up with a tally system or to compare "bad show" résumés. Rather, it's to start raising your awareness of what you're consuming and how it affects you. It's why some people take breaks from social media and some quit it altogether. In the end, if you cut out just one show that is detrimental to your spirit and your mental health, I think that's a win. It's a process. It's a sanctification journey. It's worth it.

⌐

We're spiritual beings. There's no getting around that. We're also physical beings. There's no getting around *that*. My heart, then, in these last three chapters has been to show you what you can do to attack your anxiety, your OCD, and your mental health issues in a complete manner.

I know for some of you, this chapter may have been a little more difficult, not because you necessarily disagree with me, but because the church has traditionally treated this as *just* a spiritual issue and so you tend to recoil from conversations about it. I get it. Some of you have deep scars from the way it's been handled by the church and people of faith in your life. I have some of those too. But hopefully you've seen how mental health and spirituality are connected and how, when approached correctly, their interconnectedness is not something to run from but something to press into.

As for those scars, that's why I needed to write the next chapter. It's meant for the church in general, but it's also meant for you, the sufferer. I want you to see how we can work together to call the people of God (especially those in leadership) to something better, something more complete.

CHAPTER 7

A PRESCRIPTION FOR THE CHURCH

WAY BACK IN THE INTRODUCTION I came clean about something, and I need to reiterate it here. I told you what I am not. I'm not a counselor, I'm not a theologian, and I'm not a pastor. Believe it or not, that hasn't changed in the last six chapters.

While I don't have a seminary degree, what I do have are a lot of experiences and observations. Those are what I want to share with you here. I'm not going to lie, this chapter has given me a lot of anxiety, because I want to be respectful. I also don't have all the answers. So I thought about just skipping this entire subject. But no matter how many times I took it out, I kept coming back to it. I want to write it. I need to write it. Not out of any sort of anger at the church, but because I love her, because I want to help her. Because I want her to do and be better.

And on mental health, the church can definitely do and be better.

The Diagnosis

Robert Duvall has had an incredible career in Hollywood. He's starred in everything from *The Godfather* to *Lonesome Dove*. Not surprisingly, he's been nominated for seven Academy Awards, winning once in 1984. At one point he was even named the world's most versatile actor by Guinness World Records.

That versatility was on full display for his Oscar-nominated role in *The Apostle*, a movie that might as well have been a documentary about my hometown and one of the churches I attended growing up. Duvall played the leading man, a charismatic—yet troubled—Pentecostal preacher named Sonny Dewey who finds out his wife is cheating on him; he gets drunk, beats her lover to death, and then creates a fake identity so he can start over as a preacher in another town. I can't fully explain why, but for some reason it was one of the rare non-Christian films allowed in our household. My parents were sticklers about what movies we could see. If it wasn't faith-based or on the Feature Films for Families list, we really didn't watch it.* Exceptions were made for the occasional historical movie, which meant as a teenager I could recite almost every line from *Apollo 13*.† But that was about it. TV? My sister and I once got grounded for not turning off *Full House* while stuck in a hospital waiting room.

But *The Apostle* doesn't fit into any of the "safe" categories. Sure it was *about* faith—kinda. But it was filled with cheating, beating, killing, and lying, all things that never dared grace the flickering screen of our television set. On top of that, it didn't paint Pentecostal preachers in the best light—you know, with all that cheating, beating, killing, and lying going on.

In the churches I grew up in, the pastor was treated as nearly infallible and almost untouchable. He was revered, feared, and cheered. Duvall's character wasn't any of those. He was disgraced, even if he did find redemption in the end. But, boy, could he preach. He was a gifted orator. *Anointed* was the word thrown around a lot for preachers like him when I was growing up, and he could whip a crowd into a frenzy

---

* Any other *Seasons of the Heart* or *The ButterCream Gang* people here? *Rigoletto*, anyone?
† We also all went to the theater together to see *Titanic*. Although imagine my parents' shock and horror during the nudity scene they didn't know was coming. I think that's the last movie we ever attended as a family.

in a heartbeat with a well-placed "Can I get an amen?" That's the type of preaching I was used to, and maybe that's why my parents let it slide.

I hadn't thought of *The Apostle* for decades until a couple years ago when a friend drew my attention to a sermon video posted on Facebook. It was from a small-town, charismatic Pentecostal preacher. Once I started watching it, it felt like a scene right out of the movie.

The preacher, who subscribes to the type of theology I grew up with, was talking about how Jesus came to set us free from sin. To make his point, he went through a list of captivating sins, things like anger and addiction. But he didn't stop there. He quickly veered into some all-too-familiar territory, jumping from addiction to depression and ultimately anxiety. With each word his pace quickened and his voice reached a crescendo. I could tell where he was headed, and as he continued I felt my heart beating faster and faster. Our pulses likely synced for a moment (but for different reasons) when he finally boomed his emphatic point: counseling and medication can never fix problems that aren't physical but spiritual. Especially when what's at the heart of those problems is sin.

Here's how he put it:

> People say, "Well, you need counseling to see what it is from your past. . . . Or perhaps you need some mood-altering medication and that will fix it." But to fix something you need to know what the problem is. And in Jesus's mind, there was one problem: it's called sin, and people are captive to sin and He came to set the captives free! Can I hear an "amen"?

Everything down to the call for an amen was like I was sitting in my living room in 1998 watching *The Apostle*. It also transported me back to the many sermons that accompanied those amens, sermons about having enough faith and believing yourself out of your present circumstance.

I caught myself shaking my head, partly because of the over-the-top, Hollywood-esque delivery, partly because of the theology. But mostly because it reminded me of the type of thinking that has crept through the back door of so many churches. That thinking at its worst treats mental health struggles as purely spiritual problems that only require spiritual answers, dismissing the physical aspects altogether. At its best, it still severely downplays or diminishes anything outside the spiritual. It's a type of thinking that isn't relegated to one denomination or type of church. No, it's everywhere.

Let me give you an example.

I have a good friend, Matt, who was struggling in the summer of 2020 as coronavirus cases surged in Texas, where we live. He had never struggled with anxiety before in his life, but the pandemic brought on a paralyzing fear that he would get the disease and, even though he was young and wasn't particularly at risk, he would become the exception and die from it. With every report of increased cases, Matt was struggling, and struggling hard. Because this was so new, he didn't know what to do. He called me to talk about it, hoping I could help him make sense of what was going on.

Now Matt is about as far as you can get from the "name it and claim it" branch of Christianity I've wrestled with. He falls into the Reformed camp, meaning you would never catch him attending a church where a sermon like the one I mentioned earlier is the norm. In what can only be called a strange irony, though, he and that pastor share an underlying assumption—even though Matt may not realize it. Despite facing debilitating anxiety, Matt had a hard time bringing himself to go see a counselor for his issues, and he had an even harder time calling his doctor to see if medication might be in order. Why? Because, he told me, he felt like he wasn't having enough faith, that he wasn't trusting the Lord. He felt guilt and shame, almost as if asking for and seeking help outside of anything spiritual was sinning. Sound familiar? It's essentially the core of the earlier pastor's sermon. Both of them were treating anxiety as if it were only a spiritual problem that required only a spiritual answer.

"I know it doesn't make sense," Matt admitted to me, depressed, confused, and ashamed.

You know what I told him? It absolutely does make sense that he'd be reluctant to ask for help, because that thinking is rampant. It's the type of attitude I encountered growing up, and I still see it within so many churches today. It isn't a Pentecostal problem or a Baptist problem or a Presbyterian problem. It's a church-wide problem, a Christianity-wide problem. We need to call it out, root it out, and cut it out.

When the church treats mental health issues as *only* a spiritual problem, disconnected from the brain and the body, it fails the people it is called to serve.

Remember the young woman with an eating disorder from the previous chapter? Can you imagine if we had treated her issue as purely spiritual? She would probably be dead. Really, that's what we eventually heard from her treatment team. She was on the verge of forced hospitalization because her body was so depleted. Certainly there is a spiritual component to that type of eating disorder. But it is not the only component. In fact, that's exactly what her counselor—who was a Christian—was saying when she refused to see the young woman until she got physical nourishment. Because until that happened, she could never properly address the spiritual component. But the church has done the opposite for decades by approaching mental health issues like anxiety, OCD, and depression as purely matters of the spirit and not recognizing any relation to the brain and the body.

So where does that type of thinking come from? I don't pretend to have all the answers to that question. Really, it might require a doctoral thesis to fully unpack it. But I do have some inclinations, which have come from being both a sufferer and an observer.

First, I believe the prosperity gospel has tentacles that extend far wider and deeper than we realize. The prosperity gospel embraces the idea that if you believe for something hard enough—that if you have enough faith—you can speak whatever you want into existence. It also makes *you* the decider of what is good for you instead of God. (The

Word of Faith movement I talked about earlier is a type of prosperity gospel.) This type of thinking reduces God to a vending machine: if I put in the correct change, I can pick what He gives me—good health, lots of money, success, and the like. That's why so often there is shame attached to seeking physical help for these issues, because people feel like they're not putting in the right change or have messed something up so bad that God is withholding good things from them. That teaching has also convinced so many that by turning *toward* counseling or medication, they are turning *away* from God. But that's a lie. It's a false choice. It's not an either/or: either medication *or* God. It's a both/and: you can take medication *and* have faith in God. Ironically, by treating it as an either/or, we're putting our own limits on God, telling Him how He has to work, and denying that He may help us by using common graces like medicine.

Second, we live in a time where individualism is rampant. Especially in America, where we have adopted a "pull yourself up by your bootstraps" mentality. Work hard enough at something you want and it will happen. Just look at the sayings that dominate coffee mugs, shiplap signs, and bumper stickers, including phrases like, "She believed she could so she did." And yet that's an awful way to treat your spiritual life. In fact, it's the exact opposite of what it means to be a Christian. Christianity's slogan might as well be, "She knew she couldn't so she turned to God for help." But that doesn't fit too well on a sterling silver bracelet, and it definitely won't get you sales on Etsy.

Finally, that kind of thinking comes from fear. That may seem counterintuitive. "How is refusing to acknowledge any means of help outside of prayer and faith a sign of fear?" you may ask. "Wouldn't it be the opposite? Isn't it a fear that God will not come through that makes you seek an alternative like medicine?" First of all, no, for all the reasons mentioned in chapter 4. The fear I'm talking about is deeper. It's the kind of fear that says, "What if God doesn't take this away from me? What if I pray, and believe, and pray, and believe, and I'm *still* like this? Then what?" It's a fear that your faith will be proven to be either inadequate or fake.

And it's a fear of giving up complete control—of resigning yourself to pursuing whatever options God has provided, and if you continue to have struggles, you'll have nowhere else to turn, no options left to pursue. Do you know how scary it is sometimes to be taking medication, to be seeing a counselor, to have changed my diet and exercise program, and to *still* have obsessive thoughts, panic attacks, and bouts of depression? It can be terrifying, especially because there's nothing left. That's when I'm forced to absolutely trust God that He's working, that this is His plan, and I have to rest in that. Because I'm doing everything I possibly can, I'm forced to trust Him more.

A few years ago I had a conversation with a pastor who was struggling with debilitating anxiety. After about an hour of listening to him, it became clear to me that he needed to address the physical aspects first in order to address any of the spiritual work that needed to be done. I told him he should consider talking to his doctor about medication. He looked at me and said, "I don't know, man. I don't want to do that because I don't want to be on medication for the rest of my life."

I shot back, "Whoever said you were going to be on medication for the rest of your life? But you know what, even if you do end up on medication for the rest of your life, what if that's the relief the Lord is providing for you? And isn't the Lord sovereign over that?"

He eventually agreed to go on medication, and the difference in his life was visible to all those around him.

What does that show? He had a fear of what God's answer to his struggle would be. He didn't want that answer to be medication. He was essentially saying to God, "Take this cup from me in any way but medication. That's the one thing I don't want."

We'll get into this more in the next chapter, but it's the tyranny of the "What if?" The fear is, "What if I have to take medication for anxiety for the rest of my life?" The answer: So what? If medication is the tool God has given you to fight this battle, then you need to thank and praise Him for it, not question His methods.

This fear is the same fear that my friend Matt experienced—the fear that turning to medication demonstrates a lack of faith or trust in

God. But as we talked about earlier, that's wholly inaccurate. In fact, sometimes exploring all the options—exhausting all the resources and stretching yourself thin—requires *more* faith, not *less*. Think about that for a minute.

The Prescription

So we've talked about the diagnosis (how the church has been treating mental health issues as only spiritual issues), but what about the prescription? Where does the church go from here? What can it do to better help those battling mental health issues? As I've thought about my experiences and the conversations I've had with others, it comes down to these five things:

- Introduce prayers of lament
- Teach a proper theology of suffering
- Recognize mental health issues and don't be afraid of them
- Point those suffering upward
- Point those suffering outward

Let's take each one individually.

Prayers of Lament

I am convinced that unless someone battling mental health has a proper understanding of prayer and specifically prayers of lament, that person will never find rest. Yet many churches rarely preach lament. Pastors are more than willing to do a "summer blockbuster" series where they repurpose the name of the latest Marvel movie, but they rarely delve into one of the most important tools we have in dealing with not only mental health issues but also all forms of suffering. Sure, they say a prayer before the sermon and offer a benediction, but they never go into depth about some of the most common prayers we see in the Psalms: laments. In fact, there is an entire book of the Bible devoted to laments. It's called *Lamentations*. When's the last time you heard a sermon series on Lamentations?

Laments are cries to God to be true to His word. They are born out of pain, hurt, frustration. They are deeply personal. Isaiah lamented. David lamented. Job lamented. Jesus lamented on the cross.

Look at this prayer of lament from Psalm 13:

How long, O LORD? Will you forget me forever?
How long will you hide your face from me?
How long must I take counsel in my soul
and have sorrow in my heart all the day?
How long shall my enemy be exalted over me?

Consider and answer me, O LORD my God;
light up my eyes, lest I sleep the sleep of death,
lest my enemy say, "I have prevailed over him,"
lest my foes rejoice because I am shaken.

But I have trusted in your steadfast love;
my heart shall rejoice in your salvation.
I will sing to the LORD,
because he has dealt bountifully with me.

See how heart-wrenching and personal those first two stanzas are? They are cries of pain. They are asking deep questions of God and searching for Him in the depths of extremely difficult times where the answers aren't easy to find.

There are some great resources on prayer in general from teachers like Tim Keller, Matt Chandler, and Nancy Guthrie, but what I have found to be the most helpful contribution to the topic of lament—especially for those with mental health struggles—is one I've already mentioned from author Paul Miller, *A Praying Life*. The book is packed with nugget after nugget of truth, but it's also practical and honest.

"A lament connects God's *past* promise with my present *chaos*, hoping for a better *future*," Miller explains.[1] I can't think of a better form of prayer for someone going through mental anguish. Someone who is at the end of their rope, frustrated with anxiety, tired of unceasing thoughts, or gripped with crippling depression.

But laments are a lost art. When prayer is talked about, many times it's about "asking boldly." Should we ask God to take away our struggles? Certainly. What happens if He doesn't? Then what? It's the "Then what?" the church hasn't done a good job answering. That answer? We lament. Why? Because in the process of lamenting we find the comfort and the answers we need. Look again at the last stanza of Psalm 13 above.

David just got done asking, "How long, O LORD? Will you forget me forever?" And yet by the end of the six-verse chapter he has found an answer. It may not be the answer he wanted at first, but he realizes something during the entire process of lamenting: God is sovereign, God has always been faithful, and God is working things for my good and His glory.

Too many times we treat prayer as some sort of high and rigid ritual that requires a checklist or a minimum timer. That makes it feel more like trudging through a pond of oil than it does like relaxing in a spiritual bubble bath. As I said earlier, that feeling plagued me for a long time. But what David shows us is that in prayers that come from our gut—from our heart, from places of deep pain where all we can do is muster a handful of honest sentences—God is found at the end of those prayers as well. He shows us that by asking God the simple yet tough questions, in opening ourselves up, we can experience His closeness. And he shows us that the answer to our lamenting sometimes has more to do with changing us and our perspective than changing our circumstances.

"God wants to do something bigger than simply answer my prayers," Miller writes. "The act of prayer draws God into my life and begins to change me, the pray-er, in subtle ways."[2]

Take Jesus on the cross, for example. He lamented by quoting one of the psalms of lament. You can probably recite Christ's words on the cross by heart, "My God, my God, why have you forsaken me?" (Matt. 27:46). Did you know that's the opening cry of David in Psalm 22:1?

So why would Jesus use a prayer of lament when He knew what was about to happen—when He knew death was not the final answer and resurrection was just around the corner?

Because lamenting brings us closer to God and is one of the most raw and real examples of our faith.

Again from Miller: "Laments might *seem* disrespectful, but in fact . . . lamenting shows you are engaged with God in a vibrant, living faith."[3]

By lamenting on the cross, Christ was drawing nearer to the Father. In that moment He gave us the best example of how and why to lament. That is powerful. More powerful than treating prayer and God like a vending machine. Because realizing God is with you in your suffering is what's going to sustain you "all the days of my life" (Ps. 27:4). That's the type of prayer we need to be teaching more of in the church.

A Proper Theology of Suffering

Prayers of lament are important for another reason: they lead us to a richer, deeper theology of suffering. We covered what a proper theology of suffering for us as individuals looks like in chapter 2, but we also need a proper theology of suffering corporately as the church.

I think the simplest explanation for a proper theology of suffering comes from Steven Cole, a longtime pastor in Arizona before his retirement. Ironically enough, his description comes from a sermon he delivered on David's lament in Psalm 13.

Here's what Cole says about how David eventually makes sense of his suffering: "He chose to interpret his circumstances by God's love rather than to interpret God's love by his circumstances."[4] Read that again and think about it for a minute. How often do we use our circumstances to define what God must be like instead of using what we know to be true of God to define our circumstances?

My friend Scott puts it this way in a sermon on the topic: "In other words, what David is saying here is that because of who I know God to be, what I am going through now is not the last word. What I'm going through now is not the end of the story."[5] And then he drives it all home with one of the hardest-hitting yet simple nuggets of truth I have ever heard: "Process what you don't know in the context of what you do."

That's a proper theology of suffering. We know God is good, we know He is faithful, and we know He loves us. When we face trials, difficulties, anxiety, OCD, depression, and uncertainty, we must process that through what we do know to be true about Him. You know where that leads us every time? We realize that God is using all of it for our good and His glory.

Does that mean we don't pray expectantly and fervently that God will change our circumstances or take them away? Absolutely not. Jesus in the garden of Gethsemane prayed that the Father would take away the suffering of the cross. However, we must also leave room for the fact that what we are asking may not be in line with His plan. Yet we're still told to ask. Why? Because the very act of asking brings us closer to the Father.

My little daughter, Annie, loves treats. If it's sweet, she wants it. No matter the moment or the time of day. It can be six thirty at night and she'll crawl up in my lap, put her hand on my face, raise the pitch of her voice, and say, "Daddy, I have been a really good girl tonight. Can I have a treat?" Many times I will say no because her bedtime is right around the corner, and I know what's best for her.* But in her asking, in her putting her complete trust in me that I can deliver the treat if I choose, we grow closer.

I pray often for God to remove my anxiety, my OCD, and my depression completely. So far He has not. But I have grown closer to Him as a result. Thank God.

This theology of suffering is one we need to hear from the pulpit often, pastors. Because I can guarantee you there are a lot more people in your seats struggling through trials and unanswered prayers than there are people who need to sit through a thirty-five-minute pun about the Avengers. Here's the added benefit: Those sermons do not *just* help the anxiety, OCD, or depression sufferer. They also help the husband

---

* Brett will claim I say yes more times than not. But that's not how I remember it.

who just lost his wife unexpectedly. They help the mother whose child was just diagnosed with cancer. They help the dad who just lost his job and is uncertain how he's going to provide for his family. In other words, a proper church-wide theology of suffering is ministering to those with mental health issues, for sure, but it's also ministering to every single one of your congregants who are hurting, struggling, and confused. The more you incorporate those sermons and those points, the more people you will reach. Because in the end, we're all broken and suffering from something and in desperate need of repair.

Recognizing It

Recently my twenty-year-old niece lived with our family for a time. That meant when little issues popped up with her car, I was the one she turned to for help. One day she had a headlight go out, and because she worked at a pizza place, she had to have it fixed right away so she could resume delivering food. She pulled her car into the driveway and I went to work replacing the headlight. But as I turned on her car to check my work, I noticed a warning light on the dashboard.

"Bryn, how long has this warning light been on?" I asked.

"Yikes. I don't know. A while, I think," she answered.

"Why haven't you told me or gotten it looked at?" I followed up.

"I was just kinda hoping it would go away, I guess," she responded.

We can read that and it sounds silly. You can't make something go away by simply ignoring it. Yet that's what many churches have done for a long time when it comes to mental health. It's not that they don't see it. It's that they hope with some prayer and sympathy it will just go away. But that makes about as much sense as ignoring your check engine light in hopes that it will magically turn itself off.

By the way, my niece finally took her car into the shop. It needed new brakes, a new exhaust, and some work on the starter. Those weren't going to just "go away."

Church, I understand that mental health may be scary to address and you may feel ill-equipped to deal with it. But that's no excuse not to try. Pastors, it's your responsibility as caretakers of the flock. I'm not going to pretend to have the perfect answer for what that looks like in your specific congregation. Could it be a Sunday school class you offer? Could it be a support group you create? Could it be bringing someone in to speak? Could it be simply beginning to acknowledge it in talks, discussions, and sermons? I think that's a great place to start.

In the end, what I'm hoping is that you at least take one step forward. Maybe that looks like purchasing more resources to have on hand to give out when you hear of someone struggling in your congregation.* Maybe that means acknowledging you don't know much about these issues and you need to equip yourself as a pastor or ministry leader. Whatever it looks like, please just take the next step forward. Take action. Don't just *say* you're a church that cares about people with mental health issues, *show* it. Recognizing, talking about, and acknowledging that it is there are some of the biggest steps you can take. I think one of my greatest disappointments regarding the church in general is that it has pretended that anxiety, depression, OCD, or other mental health issues either don't exist, aren't "real" issues, or aren't worth taking the time to talk about. Take the time.

As you do that, something else important begins to happen. Your church members start to feel more free to talk about *their* struggles. "People who have depression disorder, bipolar disorder, panic disorder, OCD, or any of the other mental disorders are filling your churches," Steve Bloem writes in *The Pastoral Handbook of Mental Illness* (which is an excellent resource).[6] In other words, those who struggle with mental health are in your pews. Traditionally they suffer in silence, which is why Bloem has to make it clear they're there in the first place. The more you recognize and talk openly about these issues, the more the people suffering from them will feel comfortable enough to emerge from the shadows and bring them to light. And the more they will turn to Christ and let Him penetrate that part of their lives.

---

* I'd humbly submit this book as one of those resources. But there are others, including Jennie Allen's *Get Out of Your Head*, Dena and Jason Hobbs's *When Anxiety Strikes*, and an entire conference on the subject from the Christian Counseling and Educational Foundation. See the "Further Resources" section in the back of this book for more.

I live in suburbia. One of the biggest issues I see is that people pretend everything is perfect. They project an image that is far from reality. You know what breaks down those walls? The wrecking ball of weakness. So the more the church cultivates an environment where it's OK to talk about our struggles—all of them, not just the ones people tend to be comfortable with˚—the more those struggles lose power over us.

So press into the mess. The more you do, the more your congregation will be willing to follow your lead.

Pointing Us Upward

So how do you take care of the flock once you recognize the need? It's twofold. First of all, you have to make sure to point us upward, because we have to unpack the spiritual issues that accompany our physical ones.

That means pointing us to Christ constantly. The foundational answer to making sense of our struggles—to the "Why do I have to go through this?"—is only found in Jesus.

Some of that pointing us upward is involved in the first two points: preaching prayers of lament and a proper theology of suffering. By encouraging us to bring our suffering and pain to the Lord, we are bringing it to the light. By giving a voice to the darkness, confusion, and pain within us, we start finding freedom and rest. We have to connect with the pain within us to identify it. That's when the church needs to encourage us to direct that pain to the only One who can handle it.

Beyond those, I've found particularly helpful two other concrete ways to point us upward: robust corporate worship and equipping staff members who can meet one-on-one with people who are struggling and looking for help and hope.

Richard Foster lists worship as one of the corporate disciplines. I love what he says about it: "If worship does not propel us into greater

---

* I've seen so many times when people don't mind sharing about their selfishness, their anger, or even their lust, but it's been done to make themselves appear vulnerable while hiding some of the deeper issues that really need to be brought to light and dealt with.

obedience, it has not been worship. To stand before the Holy One of eternity is to change."[7] There's something about worship that takes the focus off ourselves and puts it on Christ. When that happens, we can't help but be transformed.

Foster isn't only talking about your average Sunday morning gatherings. I'm not either. Certainly those are helpful and important, but what I'm talking about is carving out intentional gatherings that are outside of Sunday morning worship that go beyond the three or five songs and the thirty-minute sermon you can usually fit into a normal service. These "above and beyond" times, I've found, do more for pointing me to Christ and reminding me who He is and what He's done than a handful of songs on Sunday morning can because they allow for a deeper and richer immersion. That's not to say Sunday morning worship is worthless. Not at all. But it is to say you should consider special song-focused worship services from time to time (start with once a quarter, for example).

The second point isn't complicated. It flows naturally from the previous section. Equipping a specific person or people on your church staff to be fluent in mental health topics is absolutely key. Besides the obvious benefits, much of the heavy lifting when it comes to helping people suffering with mental health issues is done during one-on-one conversations, when someone struggling reaches out in a moment of crisis. Churches know how to talk about crumbling marriages or death, but they have generally failed to understand how to talk about mental health. Equipping someone to do so will allow the numerous people in your congregation who are suffering to feel heard, to feel seen, and to feel loved when they reach out or when you need to reach out to them.

If you're part of a smaller church, maybe that person is the lead pastor. If your church has more resources, maybe that looks like hiring and empowering a care pastor. Whoever it is, pick someone to be a "subject matter expert" on mental health issues and invest in them so that they can inevitably point us sufferers to Christ when the time comes. It will come.

Pointing Us Outward

The second thing the church needs to do once it recognizes mental health issues is be willing and ready to point us outward. What I mean is that the church should not shy away from directing those it's shepherding with mental health issues to seek *additional* help outside the church. That means professional counseling and professional medical advice. I want to emphasize the word *additional* again. I am not saying there is no place for the church to speak into mental health struggles. In fact, it must. It would not be the church if it didn't. However, it cannot shy away from the times when ministering to someone with mental health issues requires counseling them to get *more* help than the church is prepared or equipped to provide.

Does that mean every bout of anxiety or depression requires professional help? I don't think so. I have a friend, Brandon, who serves as a pastor in a local church. He's a former marine who has struggled with anxiety and depression since leaving the corps. He is quick to draw a distinction between episodic and clinical depression. Here's the distinction he made to me:

> *Episodic*: The "normal" feelings that happen after something tragic or significant happens, like a death in the family, a divorce, or the loss of a job.
> *Clinical*: Much bigger and much deeper. It can be cyclical at times. But there's not one thing you can point to that triggers it. It seems to come out of nowhere.

The church needs to minister to the person going through both episodic and clinical mental health challenges, but when it comes to clinical issues, the church also needs to point people outward to additional resources where it is deficient. That word *deficient* may seem jarring, but most churches are not equipped with the expertise and experience of trained mental health professionals. Is it an easy task to find the line between an episodic or clinical issue? I'm not going to pretend it is. The important tasks usually aren't. That's why I believe churches and their leadership need to seek guidance and counsel from others—authors, counselors, and mental health professionals—who have more experience in pointing people outward, to learn when it's appropriate to refer congregants to mental health experts. I also talked about some resources earlier (like Steve Bloem's book as well as the Christian Counseling and Education Foundation's entire conference on anxiety) that can guide you in helping those who are struggling. Explore them. Use them. Wrestle with them. Once again, take a step.

One final thought on pointing outward: please, whatever you do, make sure you do not belittle someone's faith who does seek supplemental help outside the church. As I said earlier, sometimes seeking outside help requires more faith and definitely more bravery, given the historic mentality of the faith community. Applaud them, support them, and love them. Don't shame them.

Look Around

In the spring of 2019, I was hosting a podcast for actor Kirk Cameron. As a result, I got to interview a plethora of interesting movers and shakers, an NFL Hall of Famer, and numerous authors. One of those authors was a young man named Ben Courson. Ben is an energetic, charismatic millennial pastor and the head of an organization called Hope Generation. He's the kind of guy whose energy is so infectious you could run through a brick wall and not feel a thing after you talk to him. And while we may differ on some things, I enjoy our conversations and love his willingness to open up about his struggles.

One of those struggles has been depression. Severe depression. The kind that cripples you.

"During my own long fight with despair I hated waking up in the morning to face another day," he writes in his book *Optimisfits*. "I would drag myself out of nightmares every morning to find no relief in waking. My future stretched out before me as an infinite grayness, with nothing to look forward to that I could actually take any joy in."[8]

What a description. So why do I tell you about Ben? Because Ben is a pastor. And if depression can happen to him—a God-fearing, "happy" person—you can bet it's happening to people throughout your congregation. You know how else I know it is? Because it's happened to people you would never expect. People like Charles Spurgeon, Winston Churchill, Martin Luther King Jr., and Abraham Lincoln. In fact, in her Pulitzer Prize–winning book on Lincoln and leadership, Doris Kearns Goodwin writes, "During a bleak winter in 1840, thirty-two-year-old Abraham Lincoln fell into a depression so profound that his friends feared he might kill himself. They confiscated all knives, razors, and scissors from his room."[9]

Likewise, what exactly do you think was happening with David when he cried out, "Why are you cast down, O my soul, and why are you in turmoil within me?" (Ps. 42:5). If that's not a description of depression, I don't know what is.

The point? You don't just need to recognize that mental health issues are happening in your pews. You need to look around and actively see who may be suffering and how you can speak into their lives. There are so many people like me, like Lincoln, and like David who need to be shepherded. That's why it's so important for the church to get this right, for the church to understand how to minister to people with mental health struggles like anxiety, OCD, and depression. We're all around, and we need you.

CHAPTER 8

AN ONGOING BATTLE

I SAID SOMETHING IMPORTANT IN the introduction: I told you this book isn't written by someone who has gotten over his struggles and is writing to you about his past issues. No, I *am* you. I still struggle.

This chapter, then, is meant to show you what that looks like. It's meant to show you that when you think you have it "under control," many times that is when you have to be most vigilant. My issues—your issues—come up again and again. And again. That's not meant to discourage you. It's meant to encourage you. It's normal. You are not broken beyond repair just because after experiencing a season on the mountaintop you find yourself in one of the deepest valleys. Maybe one day you will stay on top of that mountain. I hope so. But until then, understand that this is an ongoing battle. Let me show you what that looks like and give you some practical tips on how to live in that reality while also combating the lies.

⌐⌐

I've always loved Christmas. And really the Christmas season. I feel like there's something different that even the most callous person experiences from at least Thanksgiving to New Year's.* People are friendlier, lights are brighter, and time is slower. I haven't experienced many Christmas seasons I regret. But Christmas 2019 is one of them.

My in-laws' lake house, where I've written most of this book, is about an hour and a half away from where we live. It's become a serene retreat for all members of the family. But that December it was anything but.

Brett and I had planned on spending two weeks at the house with our kids, the week of Christmas and the week of New Year's. We had been looking forward to it for months. Brett has her own interior design business and needed the time away from clients, projects, and deadlines. I was facing some changes in my job that were causing my anxiety to flare up, so I needed the time to stare at the water with no responsibilities or expectations.

But I made a big mistake.

Given that it was winter, there were plenty of "bugs" flying around. I'm not talking about the kind that have wings. I'm talking about the kind you can't see that invade your lungs and keep you up coughing and sniffling at all hours of the night. A couple weeks before Christmas, I caught one. It knocked me out and put me in bed for a couple days. Because one of our nieces who is the recipient of a heart transplant was going to be there, I had to get on some medication to make sure I kicked it quickly, so I wouldn't be contagious. Not only was I given prescription cough medication that included narcotics, but I was also given an antibiotic. It was *a lot* of medicine.

So I decided to play doctor.

Because I was taking so many cough medications, I thought that my liver needed a break. I didn't want to be on narcotic cough meds, an antibiotic, *and* my normal anxiety and OCD med. So I decided to stop taking the anxiety medication, since in my mind it was the least pressing. We were going someplace to relax, after all.

Bad idea.

---

* I'm personally a "Christmas starts on November 1" kinda guy.

By the time we got to the house for Christmas, I had already been off it for about a week and a half.* I wasn't contagious, but I was still coughing so profusely that I needed the narcotic so I (and others around me) could at least get some sleep at night. I had no plans on taking my mental health medication during that time. I didn't even bring it with me. That's when it started.

Very early on, I started realizing something was different. Things that hadn't bothered me for years began to bother me. Conversations that had been easy started becoming hard again because I couldn't "get over" little perceived wrongs that had been done to me over the previous days. It kept building. One week into what was supposed to be our two-week stay, I pulled the plug. My wife and I packed up the family a week early and headed home. The serene had been replaced by the surreal.

"Pulling the plug" makes it seem abrupt. It was. It also makes it seem painless. It wasn't. There were tears. There was confusion on the part of my in-laws. There was frustration. In the end, leaving was better for everyone involved than experiencing the spiral I was in. See, one of the things my Prozac helps me maintain is a sense of stability. Without it, I become volatile. Not in the violent sense. I don't yell, punch walls, or anything like that. But my mood becomes less stable. That's exactly what happened there. I became agitated. Things that I was normally able to let slide became monumental issues I couldn't ignore. Simple annoyances became massive difficulties. With no medication, I was unable to get over them despite my best coping mechanisms. Remember, that's what medication has done for me. I don't treat it as a cure-all, but it does allow me to approach the world as a more "normal" person—as someone who can experience "normal" situations and make more rational and "normal" decisions.

I tell you that story so you can see exactly what I mean when I say my anxiety and OCD are ongoing battles. I am not cured. I am not healed. I have not "kicked" them or "defeated" them. I am not writing

---

* Most anxiety and depression meds take ten to fourteen days to filter through your system, so I was right at the cutoff for feeling the effects, or lack thereof.

a book on these topics because I have completely overcome them. They are ever present. They are real. I pray one day I will be made completely whole, but whether that happens tomorrow or in eternity, I can't control it. Until then, I need to put in the work. I need to take my medication.

To some that may sound defeatist. It's actually freeing. It goes back to the issue of pride and trust we talked about in chapter 6. I find more rest by realizing my limitations than I do in pretending I have none. There's a difference between rest and forgetfulness. Rest doesn't mean I have forgotten how I am wired, what my predispositions are, and the precautions I need to take for my own health. That would be living in an alternate reality. Recognizing that, though, doesn't mean it's always going to be easy to deal with. That's why I want to offer some practical advice on fighting the ongoing battle.

The Smaller Picture

Often we hear that when we take our focus off the big picture, we get caught up in the minutiae and the details and we get tripped up. In a lot of instances that is exactly right, like in a marriage relationship or even a job. But it also doesn't mean it's true all the time and in every situation.

There certainly are times when I, as someone with anxiety and OCD, get laser-focused on something small and I obsess about it and it takes over. But I've also realized that I can tend to get caught up in the bigger picture. What I mean is that sometimes the goal of being "free" from my disorder becomes so overpowering that I lose sight of the small steps, the day-by-day wins, and the little victories. Sometimes I get so obsessed with, *Why can't I just stop worrying?* or *When will this end?* that I forget about the importance of the smaller steps.

In other words, part of the ongoing battle of anxiety and OCD for me has been learning to focus on the smaller picture.

Let me give you an example. When I write, I tend to write in chunks. I'll tackle an idea, get it out on paper, and then take a break. I marinate a little bit in what I wrote and then start thinking about how to connect that to other thoughts, principles, and ideas. That looks like me getting up and walking around a little, maybe grabbing a drink, or sometimes checking a score. Today, just as I was writing this, I took one of those breaks. My distraction of choice was shopping for something on Amazon. Because I'm writing this from the porch with windows behind me, Brett could see. She popped her head out and said, with a little sarcasm, "How's that book writing coming, huh?"

I instantly got defensive.

"I'm just taking a little break. Geez."

After she went back inside, I could feel the obsessive, intrusive thoughts start.

Does she think I'm not taking advantage of this time?

Why did she have to put it like that?

Why did she disrespect me like that?

Am I wasting time?

Am I doing enough?

How can I get her to see that I'm making progress?

Have I let her down?

I've been trained to identify obsessive thoughts and potential anxious episodes. I quickly saw what was starting to happen. However, sometimes when I'm able to identify them, another issue pops up: I start obsessing about having obsessive thoughts.

Why can't I stop thinking about this?

Why am I this way?

Why has this taken up so much of my time?

When will this end?

In those times, I go to another technique. I narrow my focus. I make the picture smaller. So instead of letting my thoughts continue to fester, I decided to make a conscious effort to refocus my mind. I got up, took a quick minute to stretch, sat back down, and gave myself a goal to type out a few hundred words. You know what? By the time I'm writing this now, my perspective has changed, my mind is clearer, and I'm no longer bogged down by the earlier interaction.

That's a small win. And one I can build on. But if I were to let my mind focus on the bigger goal of just wanting to stop thinking about this, I would not have gotten here so quickly. It could have been hours of ruminating, leading to a lot of frustration. Instead, I focused on giving myself a small victory, and in doing so found relief a lot quicker.

Big, massive goals are great for a lot of things, but for people like us who obsess and let our minds wander to about three thousand possible ways to get there, sometimes the best thing to do is to take a step back and focus on the more immediate needs and the little ways we can achieve our bigger goal.

Battling anxiety isn't about imagining a life without it. It's about finding small victories that get me to a place where I'm properly aligning my worries with the small truths of God's Word and His promises.

Remember when we talked about meditation earlier? Focusing on the smaller picture is the littler brother of meditation (and also mindfulness), just much less formal. It's consciously finding the small nugget that lets you refocus your mind and get out of the endless thought cycle.

Battling the Tyranny of "What If?"

If you've had anxiety for any length of time, you've experienced the question that drives the ongoing battle. It's a question that leads to frantic thoughts and frenetic actions. A question that contains a lot of fear, especially for being only six letters long. That question is, "What if?"

What if my wife not wanting to have sex means she doesn't find me attractive and wishes she never married me?

What if my husband not answering his phone means he's cheating on me?

What if my boss not returning my call right away means he's upset, disappointed, or wants to fire me?

What if my colleague reads that email in a tone other than what I intended?

What if we aren't able to sell our house for what we're asking? What if we have to take a loss?

What if that noise I heard under my car was a person and not a bump?
What if that table is covered with germs and I get sick?
What if that cough means something is seriously wrong?
What if that noise I hear from my car means a costly repair?
What if I don't have enough money to do that repair?
What if I'm not able to get all this work done before the end of the day?
What if, what if, what if?

I call it the tyranny of the "What if?" For anxious people, it is the ever-present question in the back of our minds. That's why we have to combat it with a different question. A question rooted in trust. That question is, "So what?"

Those two words—"So what?"—are crucial. We anxiety sufferers have an inordinate fear of what *might* happen. We run through numerous possibilities in our heads until we grab hold of one that seems plausible (even if ridiculous) to us, and then we replay it over and over and over again. But by asking ourselves, "So what?" we strip the "What if?" of its power. The "So what?" forces us to think a little more rationally, a little more logically.

"So what happens if [*insert feared outcome*] actually comes true? Will it be as bad as I think?" The answer is almost always, "No!"

That's not to say there aren't times when the answer to the "What if?" can be hurtful and detrimental. For instance, if you have an inordinate fear of your spouse cheating on you, and it actually does come true, you'll understandably be devastated. So how should "So what?" comfort you in that scenario? Well, you have to go a step further and turn the question into a statement: "So what?" becomes "So what!" In other words, the hurt, the pain, the hardship that comes can't be more powerful than the God who has it all under control.

"So what! God has me!"

That admittedly sounds a little trite, but here's my point: if you truly grasp the truths that God loves you and that He's really working things for your good, then you can—you have to—rest in that.

Still, the truth is that for every one time the answer to our "What if?" is actually the worst-case scenario we imagined, there are tens of thousands of other times where it is not. I don't have to tell you that. You already know it.

Generally, then, the "So what?" is never as bad as the "What if?" Remind yourself of that as often as you need to.

By the way, "What if?" and "So what?" contain the same number of letters, with only two of them being different: "so" and "if." I'll ask a different question, then: Which two letters are you going to let control you?

The Unexpected Battles

Sometimes you feel like you may be winning the anxiety battles. You may feel things are under control, but then something comes up out of the blue. Maybe there's an event (a death in the family, for example) that thrusts you into a fight you thought you had won or forces you to confront something you never expected to face. Friend, I've been there.

A few years ago, I faced something I had never experienced before. I was overseeing a digital media project that at the time required some difficult decisions that would affect the employee working under me. She was a great person, contributed a lot to our success, and had gone through a hard time personally in recent months. Despite trying to avoid it, it was becoming clear that her job was no longer sustainable on our shrinking budget.

It was tearing me up. I respected her and her husband a lot. We had become friends and yet I was going to have to let her know that she no longer had a job during one of the toughest periods of her life. To make matters worse, she had recently told me she was pregnant.

It sent me to a dark place. I began going to bed earlier and earlier, sometimes by six o'clock. What brought me happiness in the past could now barely spark a reaction. My marriage began to suffer. I became closed off, easily agitated, frustrated, and, quite frankly, frustrating. A fog seemed to take over. I remember one evening leaning over our kitchen counter and just staring down, my face as blank as my mind. Brett turned the corner and asked me what was wrong.

"I don't know. I really don't. I just feel numb and emotionless."

And that's when I realized it. It was the proverbial light bulb moment.

"I feel . . . depressed," I said. The words were hard to get out, but once I finally said it, a weight seemed to lift. Not the full weight. More like a five-pound dumbbell. It was just enough to give me a little relief and, more importantly, give me clarity for what I needed to do.

That night, I emailed my counselor, Mike, to set up an appointment. That was on a Saturday. By Monday I was sitting in front of him and trying to explain what I had been experiencing the last two months. Since he's a good counselor, he didn't tell me the "answers" but rather asked me good questions that led me to the truths I already knew.

And do you know what type of questions he asked me? He asked me a lot of "So what?" ones.

So what if you lose your job? Do you think God is not going to take care of you?

So what if you have to tell your employee that her job is going away? Have you done all you can do to try to save it? Do you think that even if it's difficult, she can hear and understand that?

So what exactly do you think defines you: what you do or who you are and who God says you are?

Each question pulled me further and further out of the depths of despair as I meditated on who God is, what He's promised, and how I know I can trust Him.* Mike could have charged me five hundred dollars for that session and it would have been worth every penny.

⌇

That depression battle is something I never expected to face. Remember, I (inaccurately) thought years ago that because I'm a happy, jovial person I was immune. I'm not. You're not. The truth is sometimes we

---

* That doesn't mean my depression ended right then and there. No, there was still work to be done. However, those questions were pivotal in reversing the downward trend and giving me hope.

face battles we never thought we were going to have to fight. When those battles present themselves, don't be surprised if you think you can't handle them. I'm here to tell you, though, that you can.

It's OK if you're tired of fighting the battle and just wish it was healed, cured, and over with. I've been there. It's OK if you're feeling thrown for a loop that the battle looks different now than it did last year or even last month, and you wish it would at least just stay the way you know and have learned to manage. I've been there too. It can be a harsh reality that our mental health struggles continue despite medication, despite counseling, and despite the support of friends and loved ones. But please know that that doesn't mean we don't have the practical tools, the help, and the grace we need to keep fighting the battle.

Also know that the truths we've talked about in this book apply to anxiety, OCD, depression, death, addiction, and a myriad of other struggles. I'm not saying you shouldn't seek out help and resources specific to your issue, but what I am saying is that many of the tools we've talked about thus far are at minimum a good start. When an intruder finds you unprepared in your house, feel free to use the baseball bat in the closet instead of waiting for the perfect tool to fight back.

CHAPTER 9

HELP ME UNDERSTAND

THIS CHAPTER ISN'T FOR THE actual anxiety sufferer, although if that's you, I still think you need to read it because it will help you help those who love you (and there's also something special for you at the end). It's for the husband who feels like he's walking on eggshells with his wife. It's for the wife who can't figure out why her husband is so "touchy." It's for the person who doesn't understand why their best friend went from being so sociable to never wanting to go out. It's for the brother, sister, and in-law who either has seen their family member become someone different or can't quite figure out why they're always "on edge."

As much as I needed to name what was going on inside of me so I could understand it, Brett and those around me needed me to name it so they could start understanding me as well. The problem, though, is that while there are guidebooks and maps for the anxiety sufferer (hence this book), when it comes to those around the sufferer, instead of giving them a map, society tends to give them a Google satellite view with all the roads removed. In other words, they have a general idea of what's going on but they have absolutely no idea about where to go or how to proceed.

I remember after one particularly difficult stretch with an anxiety flare-up and some tears from Brett, she retreated to an early bedtime. I sat on the couch and whispered to myself, "Your anxiety, your insecurities, your constant questioning can be so exhausting to other people."

And that's exactly how she felt, and still sometimes feels. Does that sound familiar? Does it sound unromantic? I hope so. Because life isn't a Hallmark movie or a Nicholas Sparks book. The truth is, the people around us anxiety sufferers can get really tired and feel really hopeless at times. That's why I'm writing this chapter. I want you—the friend or family member, the pastor, the support system—to have hope. Here we go.

Understanding What Anxiety Is

I'm going to take a little bit of a risk here, but I think it's worth it. I'm going to define "anxiety" simply and concisely. That's not to say it isn't complex, but it's best to start at the core and then move to the more complex in order to understand something. There has to be a foundation before there can be an attic, and the foundation is exactly what I want to lay.

So here it goes: anxiety is an inordinate fear of the unknown.*

That's it. Before you dismiss that explanation, take a moment to think about it. It makes sense, doesn't it? The anxiety sufferer you know is absolutely terrified of uncertainty. They can't stand not knowing what's going to happen, not knowing why something happened, not knowing what someone's thinking, not knowing where they stand, and so on. They don't like to take risks because risks have uncertain outcomes. So they play it safe. They crave comfort and predictability. A + B = C, and it's a beautiful thing.

In order to understand anxiety, you have to realize that psychologically the person suffering from it is craving safety. That's because an anxiety disorder is the result of your brain not reacting correctly to fight-or-flight signals.

---

* And remember from chapter 1, OCD is a form of coping with that fear.

Anxiety.org explains it well: "An anxiety disorder results when the flight or fight response becomes triggered too easily and too frequently. Usually, this occurs after many events of any kind that are perceived as threatening from early childhood to the present or fewer extremely intense events that have left a strong impression of danger on the individual. As a result, the brain has learned to perceive the world as more dangerous than it actually is. In the most serious anxiety disorder, panic disorder, the individual's physiologic response is genuine terror."[1]

In other words, an anxiety disorder is when the brain can't properly filter out the real versus the unreal threats and goes into overdrive. It's why panic attacks are treated with "downers," or drugs that calm you, because when the fight-or-flight response is all haywire, your heart races, your mind wanders, and you want to fight or run even in situations where you are physically and emotionally safe.

Does that sound like your friend or loved one? Always on edge, high-strung, constantly afraid?

The other thing that's important to understand about anxiety sufferers is that once we do move on from one fear, we are quick to find another. I can't tell you how many times I've laid in bed at night after a good, peaceful, restful day only to have my mind start searching for something to be wrong.

You're a little too calm right now. Are you sure there's nothing you should be thinking or worrying about? Are you sure you didn't miss something? This seems too good to be true.

For most anxiety sufferers, anxiety is their normal state of being. So when things get too peaceful or too calm, it feels odd. It's abnormal. It's weird and different. And we start searching for what we know best: chaos and uncertainty.

You may be starting to have some epiphanies right about now. I hope so. This is why you can be experiencing a great time with your friend, loved one, or spouse and seemingly "out of nowhere" some issue, some worry, pops up. It's because we anxiety sufferers tend to be more comfortable in a state of anxiety. Not because we enjoy it, but because that's what our bodies and brains are used to—and the mere thought of not having anything to worry about makes us worry. That's why we tend to have a harder time unplugging, going on vacations, and truly "relaxing and unwinding" like you can.

It Isn't Always a Bad Thing

The way I just described anxiety may be scary for some—both the sufferer and the loved one. But I don't want you to be defeated. Remember, there is hope. In fact, anxiety isn't always a bad thing. I think one of the most helpful and important realizations for me came when I understood that anxiety and OCD have some benefits.

When I went to my psychiatrist for the first time, he told me that everyone has a little anxiety and OCD. That at first might sound like a little bit of an exaggeration, but I think I now understand what he was getting at. That doesn't mean everyone is walking around battling what I have. No, what I think he was saying is that there are normal aspects of anxiety and OCD inside each and every one of us. They rise to the level of a diagnosis when they are out of control. When the normal, accepted levels become abnormal and life-altering.

I like to think of it this way. Have you ever taken the time to look at the list of the seven deadly sins? OK, probably not. But I want you to take a look now and tell me if you realize anything: lust, gluttony, greed, sloth, wrath, envy, pride.

Do you see it? The seven deadly sins are all an excess of something good. In other words, they are an abnormal amount of something originally meant to be helpful, useful, and necessary. Maybe this will help. Take a look at the sins' healthy counterparts: romance, nourishment, making a living, rest, justice, drive, self-confidence.

That second list is filled with things that are either natural, neutral, or necessary. We need rest. We need nourishment. We should fight for justice. It's when we become consumed with them that they become bad.

When we become consumed with romance, it becomes lust.

When we gorge ourselves on food, it becomes gluttony.

When wanting to make a living turns into an unquenchable thirst for more money, it becomes greed.

When our desire for rest becomes paramount, it becomes sloth.

When we take justice into our own hands, it becomes wrath.

When we go from admiring someone's success to wanting what they have, it becomes envy.

When our self-confidence becomes all-consuming, it becomes pride.

So what does that say about anxiety and OCD? They are unhealthy versions of good principles and natural instincts.

When self-preservation and concern become all-consuming, they become anxiety.

When attention to detail and thoughtfulness completely take over, they become OCD.

In other words, the excess of the good things is what makes them bad. Remember, anxiety is an inordinate fear of the unknown, and thus an overactive fight-or-flight response to that fear. That's why it's an excess of self-preservation. Self-preservation is not, in itself, a bad thing. It's how we stay alive. You being alive is a good and noble desire.

Here's what healthy anxiety looks like. A couple years ago two buddies and I spent a week in the Alaskan bush. We had to be flown in via a floatplane. No roads. No phones. No police. No hospital. If something happened, the closest help would come via a satellite tracker ping we sent to someone in the Lower 48, who would then have to contact local authorities, who would then be a minimum of a few hours away. In other words, help wasn't coming quickly. On top of that, we were in the middle of bear country. One of my companions had made the trip the year before and saw so many bears so close you'd think they were pets. That made me anxious. That anxiety made sure I took proper precautions not to become a grizzly's dinner. That meant everything from carrying bear spray and a firearm to constant shouts of "Hey, bear!" whenever I was walking through the woods.* I'm glad I was anxious. It was a healthy anxiety, the kind that's the difference

---

* The cabin we were at didn't even have plumbing, which meant any bathroom trips in the middle of the night included a walk to the outhouse with a shotgun. Talk about anxiety!

between life and death. In other words, a lack of anxiety—or in this proper sense, a lack of self-preservation—could have been detrimental to my health.

What might healthy OCD look like in "normal" people? Well, it manifests as particularity or preference. It looks like you always and only enjoying your burger cooked medium-rare.* Having a favorite color. Liking a specific genre of music. Preferring a certain type of wine. Those are typical. They are not odd. What is odd is when those preferences become controlling, when the thought of not having those things—or having things other than those things—keeps you up at night, leads you to panic attacks, or captivates your thoughts for hours on end.

That's what happens with someone with anxiety—and specifically an OCD disorder.

Take the common example of locking your doors. We all want to be safe so we all lock our doors at night.† But the OCD person can't stop thinking about what happens if their doors aren't locked. They lock them, but later (or quickly after in some cases) when any sort of doubt creeps in about whether they locked them or not, they check and then recheck and then check some more. That's where the "compulsive" action comes in. The only way to get relief from the worry and anxiety is to act—again and again and again—or to avoid the catalyst altogether, which leads to isolation. It's OK and healthy to crave safety. It's unhealthy when it consumes you to the point of losing sleep over it.

So what are some of the healthy benefits of anxiety, and in my case OCD?

People with anxiety can be really safe people—meaning they are risk averse. Growing up, that was me, especially during my teenage and high school years. I was never the one partying, staying out late, or taking the dumb chances many teens do. Why? I was so afraid of the potential consequences. I would play out the scenarios in my head

---

* In reality, anything more done than this is cause for me to question a lot about you.
† Unless you're in those parts of Wisconsin where I grew up, or somewhere similar. My brother still leaves his keys in the visor from time to time when he goes into the store.

of what would happen if I were caught drinking or drove drunk. I remember one time during my junior year when I was at my older brother's house. Since I had planned to sleep over, he let me have two beers—two—with him that night. When I woke up the next morning, I was supposed to go meet a friend. I refused. Why? Because I was so afraid that if I just happened to get pulled over and an officer happened to smell something on my breath and gave me a Breathalyzer, he would find a trace amount of alcohol in me from the night before and I would lose my license. No lie. I stayed at my brother's until the afternoon and brushed my teeth about five times.

In other words, my anxiety kept me out of a lot of trouble in my younger years. And it still makes me particularly risk averse in my adult ones. I have never done a forward flip or a backflip into a pool. I follow the rules, generally to a tee. I have only received one speeding ticket in my life, and I was almost thirty when it happened.

Here are some of the other good things that anxiety and OCD have brought me:

- When it comes to writing—when it comes to work—I have an attention to detail that is generally unmatched. I already told you at the beginning that I reread emails a lot. Well, that means I reread what I write a lot. I catch my own errors more than most. I also respond to emails quickly, because I get anxiety with unfinished tasks hanging over my head. One colleague recently told me he's never experienced someone responding so quickly to his messages. I wear that as a badge of honor.
- I can teach myself things quickly, because the thought of disappointing a boss, a coworker, or Brett is overwhelming. I've taught myself Photoshop, video editing, and even how to install electrical outlets so I can get things done quickly and easily.
- I have the ability to connect with people almost instantly and on a deep level. Anxiety and OCD can make you empathetic, with a keen ability to recognize and think about what others are going through. During a rare family vacation in my teen years,

my mom, stepdad, and I went on a carriage ride. I love horses. I had one for a brief time growing up and still long for one to this day. I asked the driver if I could sit up front with her while she drove us around. She agreed. By the end of the ride, I had gotten her to share her life story with me. She talked about her kids, a failed marriage, and everything in between. I was thirteen. My mom remarked after the ride, "Jonny, how did you do that?" The answer? I asked pointed and open-ended questions. It's stuck with me to this day. During a long car ride with one of my friends from high school after a recent reunion trip, he turned to me and said, "Man, has anyone ever told you that you ask *really* good questions?" What can I say? I'm thorough.

- When my boss asks me for data or presentations, I don't just send the raw numbers. I put together elaborate spreadsheets or I create stimulating presentations with dynamic pictures. When I worked with Kirk Cameron, he jokingly started asking me to give him presentations with the "Jon Seidl treatment." It's become a thing.

- I care what people think of me, so it drives me to be helpful. If you need something, I usually say yes. If a boss, peer, or anyone in between needs help, I'm usually there. If something requires going the extra mile, sign me up. And I absolutely love blowing the top off expectations. It's almost intoxicating.

Does that sound like your friend or loved one at their best? I hope so, because those are good things. It's when the good things are warped or perverted that it becomes detrimental, like when the request for a presentation comes through on a Friday afternoon, and because I can't stop thinking about it—and because it has to look a certain way—I spend most of the weekend working on it at the expense of my family life and obligations.

It becomes dangerous when I send a text message and then have paralyzing fear for hours afterward wondering how it was interpreted, especially if the person doesn't respond soon after.

It becomes a disorder when a disagreement, not even an argument, with my wife in the morning ruins the entire day because I can't stop thinking about what she said, what I said, and what this will mean going forward. In a way it becomes a self-fulfilling prophecy.

That's why I say the line between anxiety and an anxiety disorder is a matter of excess. There's similar evidence about depression and its healthy counterpart, realism. Nassir Ghaemi is a professor at Tufts University in Boston. In 2011 he wrote *A First-Rate Madness: Uncovering the Links Between Leadership and Mental Illness,* a provocative book on how mental illness has a way of making us better leaders. That may be surprising to some, but given what we just talked about, I don't think it's that far-fetched. Here's what he explains about depression:

> "Normal" nondepressed persons have what psychologists call "positive illusion"—that is, they possess a mildly high self-regard, a slightly inflated sense of how much they control the world around them.
>
> Mildly depressed people, by contrast, tend to see the world more clearly, more as it is. In one classic study, subjects pressed a button and observed whether it turned on a green light, which was actually controlled by the researchers. Those who had no depressive symptoms consistently overestimated their control over the light; those who had some depressive symptoms realized they had little control.[2]

In other words, mild depression can give us a more realistic view of the world. It can show us our flaws and where we need to focus our improvement efforts. It can help us realize what we are incapable of and where we need to turn for help.

Just because your husband, your wife, your son, your daughter, your friend, your you-name-it is struggling with anxiety, OCD, or depression doesn't mean there is nothing redeemable about those issues. God is still working in them, among them, and through them. Remember the story of my grandma, someone who pretty clearly struggled with anxiety but was still able to be a calming force in my life? Your

FINDING REST

loved one's disorder is not a curse that automatically puts them at an insurmountable disadvantage throughout their life. Do you know why it's important for you to understand that? It's not just for you. It's also for us, because sometimes we sufferers can get so bogged down in our diagnoses that we can't see the silver lining of what God is doing. That's when we need you. There have been several times in our marriage where Brett has (lovingly) reminded me that I don't have to accept or live like I am a burden. I have a lot to contribute, and even in my flaws God is at work. Be ready to do the same thing.

What Not to Say (aka the Main Event)

Now that you have a better, more complete understanding of what a person with anxiety and OCD is going through and who they are, I feel a little like this section is the chapter's main event. Not that everything I've said up until this point isn't important or useful. But what I'm about to say is probably what most people are craving, even if they don't know it. It's what can lead to either the most frustration or the most relief for both parties. Master it—internalize it—and it can enrich and grow your relationship. It's the part of the chapter Brett jokingly, but also kind of seriously, titled, "Just Get Over It." And that, friends, is the first phrase not to say to someone struggling with anxiety.

"Just Get Over It"

There are several variations of this phrase.

"Just stop thinking about it."

"Relax."

"Can you just give it a break?"

"Take your mind off of it."

"Just think of something else."

And they are all even more volatile when followed by an "already." Never, under any circumstances, tell someone in the middle of an anxious period, a depressive episode, a panic attack, or an OCD cycle to "Just get over it already."

158

I'm going to do my best to explain what happens inside us when we hear that. At the risk of sounding hyperbolic or being cliché, I'll put it like this: It's like a nuclear bomb, only the atoms inside are anger, resentment, frustration, confusion, and shame. They're knocking around, splitting, and exploding. All of that eventually detonates into a mushroom cloud of tension, hurt, and dismay. I don't think there has been a more hurtful, confusing, frustrating, and yet true phrase spoken to anxiety sufferers than "Just get over it already."

Why do I say "true"? Because we *do* want to just get over it. That would solve a lot of issues. Trust me, we know. The problem is, though, we can't just grit it out and switch it off. Believe me when I say it frustrates us just as much as it frustrates you, and probably more. We know we need to drop it. We know we have to. Yet we know we can't. That's why we can get so agitated at times.

Don't Downplay It (Right Away)

One thing I will admit right off the bat is that some of what I'm saying will seem counterintuitive. This is one of those things: don't downplay what's going on, or in other words, don't try to diminish what your friend or loved one says they're struggling with.

"Don't downplay the anxiety?" you may ask. "Shouldn't that be *exactly* what I do?"

No, but let me explain.

Remember my friend Matt, the one who had never had anxiety until the coronavirus pandemic hit? When he called me to talk about what was happening, the easy thing for me to do would have been to say, "Matt, come on, man, you know that's ridiculous. You have been isolating most of the time. When you do go out you socially distance, and you aren't putting yourself in compromising situations. The stats say you are less likely to get it. And even if you do, you know that you're in the age bracket that puts the risk of serious illness very low. You're going to be OK. You don't have anything to worry about. OK?"

On the surface, that may sound like something completely reasonable to say. But for someone with anxiety—and especially in the height of an anxious episode—it feels dismissive. It feels uncaring and unloving. It comes across as belittling. Many times we anxiety sufferers know the facts. We could spit them out to you a thousand times faster than you could. But the problem isn't logical, it's emotional (and physical and spiritual).

Instead, what we need is for you to be *with* us instead of trying to *fix* us. We need you to talk *with* us instead of talking *at* us. One of the greatest weapons against anxiety is quality time spent with people who care. I'm not going to say it's like kryptonite. That's too immediate. It's more like an antibiotic: it needs to be taken regularly to get the full effects.*

Let me give you an example of talking *at* versus talking *with* that should help you make the distinction. Before a recent move I was a member of my neighborhood's local Facebook group. You know, the place where everyone goes to complain about loud booms, barking dogs, and anything else that makes a sound or mildly inconveniences them. One night we had some storms roll through our area. Lightning, thunder, everything that would get people talking. While scrolling through my feed during the storm, sure enough someone had posted a message about it. What was interesting about this message was that it wasn't a question asking if anyone had lost power or wondering about lightning flashes or even attempting to identify the latest odd noise. No, this woman decided to post a message directly to the storm itself. Yes, you read that right. She posted a message *to* the storm. It went like this: "Dear storm, thanks for waking up my pups and scaring them half to death. Oh, and thanks for the no power. That's really great."

It goes without saying, obviously the storm is never going to see it. So why even post it? Because she's looking for a response. She wants empathy. She wants to be heard. She wants to be talked *with*. She wants someone to understand her struggle.

So what, then, is the worst response to that? What is the opposite of

---

* That's why community has come up so many times already.

what she's looking for? You can probably guess. It came from someone who decided to lecture her.

"That's why you should have gotten a backup generator," the man wrote. "Always have a backup plan."

This is me rolling my eyes. That's not talking *with* her, that's talking *at* her. Is he wrong? Not necessarily. Yes, having a backup plan is always great. We should have backup plans for almost everything in life.* But there are so many other potential things at play that this man has no idea about. What about her financial situation? Her job situation? Is she renting? He doesn't know. He doesn't know because he hasn't gotten a chance to know her. He hasn't listened. And thus he hasn't earned the right to say what he said. The woman wasn't asking for advice; she was asking for an ear.

That's what the anxiety sufferer many times is asking for. We're not asking you to fix the situation, or to fix us. We're asking for you to talk *with* us about what's going on.[†]

There's a question I hope you're asking here: "If we don't challenge the thoughts or downplay what's going on, and we just let them go on thinking what they're thinking, are we giving in to the lies the disorder is telling?"

It's a great point. And an important one. I am not suggesting you need to validate the lies the disorder is telling your loved one. But you can validate the feelings without waving the white flag. In fact, there should be a time when you have a conversation about whether or not the thoughts are based in truth, where you talk about whether they are growing and taking over at an unhealthy pace. But that shouldn't be your *first* reaction. It shouldn't be your *first* conversation. Sometimes, depending on the friend or family member, it shouldn't even be your second. And that can be true not just for the relationship as a whole, but also with each individual episode.

Let me put it this way: You need to earn the right to speak truth

---

* In honor of Brett, I'm saying "almost" because we should not have a backup plan for our spouse.

† I can almost hear the collective "amen" of every married woman reading this right now.

into an anxious person's life.* After that, you need to earn the right to speak truth into an anxious person's struggle. Again, that does not mean you should ignore truth, ignore reality, and never speak of what's going on. It's become popular to elevate feelings over facts and treat the former as the be-all and end-all. But feelings should never trump facts. Still, that doesn't mean the feelings aren't the person's reality in that moment. Feelings aren't useless. In fact, feelings can tell you *a lot* about what's going on. Look at it this way: a doctor can only help someone fix an issue after that doctor listens to the symptoms, understands the pain, and does some real digging for the diagnosis and the cure. That's what I'm telling you to do.

Brett has learned, through a lot of practice, how to do this. Last summer we spent some time as a family at my in-laws' lake house. My father-in-law has a boat that he loves to take the kids on. As often as he can, we all load up and motor on over to a little cove on the water that turns into a swimming hole on the weekends. On this particular weekend, we spent an afternoon anchored near the sandy shore and jumping off the boat time after time after time until our hands were pruned and our skin was burned.

Eventually, we packed up the floaties, pulled in the anchor, and started heading back to the house. One of the kids' favorite things to do, though, is to sit on Papa's lap and drive the boat with him. As my father-in-law was getting situated for that to happen, we passed someone's dock going a little too fast and probably a little too close. You would have thought we had just buzzed the thing with an F-16 fighter jet based on the dock owner cursing us out, flailing his arms, and making gestures as if he wanted to fight us. It was an honest mistake, and at no time were we or they in danger.

But when we got back to the house, I couldn't get the incident out of my mind.

What if they had gotten in their boat and started chasing us?

---

* Generally, that's a good rule to follow for all relationships. Sometimes as Christians we can go on verbal crusades with people we barely know or haven't spent much time with. It does way more harm than good.

What if they tried to "get us back" with the kids on board?

What if they look up the boat registration number, come find us, and try to confront us?

What if . . . ?

In other words, the tyranny of the "What ifs?" began taking over. And of course it was irrational. The likelihood of someone on the opposite end of the lake hunting down a boat with toddlers was unlikely. The facts and reality were telling me that. Yet I couldn't stop thinking about it.

Later on when it was just Brett and me together, I told her I was having a hard time getting those thoughts out of my head. Her response was perfect.

"I know!" she said. "I was a little scared too. I'm not sure why that guy got so concerned. But I'm glad we're all safe, and I know that if we saw them again we'd be OK and be able to have a reasonable conversation. But yeah, I was definitely a little concerned as well."

Do you see what she did? She validated the feelings without giving in to the lies. She made me feel heard instead of alone. She didn't scoff at the ridiculousness but talked and sat *with* me.

My friend Dan and his wife have turned this concept into a little game. Dan suffers from some of the same things I do, so when he feels himself getting anxious about something, or his mind is flooded with a lie, he takes a page out of *The Hunger Games*.

In the blockbuster series, Peeta Mellark is brainwashed and tortured to the point where he can no longer decipher what's real or fake. Sometimes he even sees things that aren't there. When he's having a hard time figuring out what's real, he turns to his friend and the story's protagonist, Katniss Everdeen, and asks her a simple question: "Real or not real?" She then tells him the truth.

That's what Dan asks his wife. When he's struggling with something, he asks her if it's "real or not real" (or some variation), and she tells him the truth. It's a beautiful and concrete example of how she's earned the right to speak truth into his life, and how Dan relies on her to help him through the struggles. It also cuts to the core of his anxiety, since we sufferers have a hard time deciding between the real and the not-real threats.

I don't pretend finding that delicate balance in your relationship is always going to be easy. It takes time and trust. It's a learned process. It's going to look different for every relationship, and it's going to get messy at times. That's why I'm writing this now, to help you start that journey and start with a map instead of having to chart the course yourself.

⌒

A final word on the interaction with my friend Matt, the one who struggled with COVID-19 fear. My response to him in his moment of anxiety wasn't to verbally vomit this book at him, tell him everything I'd learned, and go through the highlights of every chapter. Instead, I listened. I told him how much "that sucks." I asked him questions about how he was feeling and what things were like at home. I let him do most of the talking. I didn't try to solve his issue right then and there. We prayed together, and then we hung up. But that conversation led to another, and another, and another. Several conversations in, I finally brought up that I thought he should see a doctor and a counselor. He listened, because I had sat with him in the mess. Today, he's on medication and is seeing a Christian counselor. I'm not sure that would have happened if that was the first thing I told him to do during our initial conversation.

What Else You *Should* Say and Do

I remember confiding in a well-intentioned person early on in my diagnosis. I was trying to figure out how all this factored into my faith. So I shared my situation with this man and at the end of the conversation he gave me a nine-word response: "I just think you need to pray about it."

Really? I thought. *That's your advice?*

I haven't confided in that person since. Not because their advice was completely wrong, but because it was so incomplete. Listen, I do need to pray about this, daily, constantly, fervently. But in that moment, in the depths of pouring out my soul, the response seemed trite. It seemed like a cop-out. It wasn't pressing into my pain; it was trying to gloss over it.

We covered that phrase in depth in chapter 6, but I bring it up again here because I don't just want to tell you what to avoid, I want to explain what you should pursue. That's why I created the chart you're about to see. I want to help you by giving some practical examples of what you should say, not just what you shouldn't.

Take the "just pray about it" example. Notice what's included in the opposite column: "Point us to biblical truths." The point is not that you avoid spiritual conversations. The point is that once you've earned the right to speak into the situation and are facing those conversations, then do it. But do it in such a way that requires you to be intentional.

If the same man who told me to "just pray about it" had instead sat with me (there's that concept again) and walked me through some of the biblical truths he has meditated on during some of his struggles and asked me some genuine questions, it would have been a much different outcome—and it would have led to a much different relationship, a better one. There's nuance here, I know. But it's important nuance.

This is not an exhaustive chart by any means, but I hope it helps guide you.

WHAT NOT TO SAY AND DO	WHAT YOU SHOULD SAY AND DO
Talk at	Talk/pray with
Downplay	Validate
Dismiss	Affirm
Repeat/nag	Redirect
Confront immediately with facts	Listen

WHAT NOT TO SAY AND DO	WHAT YOU SHOULD SAY AND DO
Try to fix it	Speak truth in time
Tell us to "just get over it"	Ask questions
Escalate	Defuse
Blame	Express how you feel
Rehash past episodes	Talk about the present situation
Tell us to "just pray about it"	Point us to biblical truths
Ask us if we've taken our meds	Ask us if we've taken our meds

By the way, it's not a typo that the last phrase in the chart is the same for both sides. I remember one time when I was getting irritable about some silly things and Brett turned to me and snapped, "Have you been taking your meds?" Let's just say that did *not* make me any less irritable. Yet there have been other times when Brett, in a loving, gentle, and concerned way, has approached me and asked, "Jon, you seem a little off lately. Have you been good about taking your meds?" Whenever she's approached it in the latter way, it's led to great discussions and deeper intimacy between us.

So what's the difference? Tone, for one. Context, for another. Body language is also a big factor. You've probably heard it before, but most communication is nonverbal. Psychologists disagree on the actual percentages (some go as high as 93 percent, while others put it lower), but the point is still clear. How you say something and how you express what you're saying says a lot more than what you're actually saying.

That said, I don't pretend that this is a simple formula that's always going to yield the desired outcome. Sometimes there are moments, incidents, and episodes that need to work themselves out. Brett and I experience those. I remember one time when I was looking for something that had fallen under the couch after I had just gotten brand-new prescription sunglasses. Even with insurance they put a dent in the proverbial pocketbook. As I got on my stomach to look for whatever it was that had fallen under the couch, I heard a crunch.

I'd forgotten that I'd hung my sunglasses on my shirt. They snapped in half.

I was so upset with myself. *Why weren't you paying attention? Where are we going to get the money to fix them or get new ones? Idiot!*

Brett did everything right in the moment. She validated the frustration and then tried to redirect it. She even planned a date for later that night to help me take my mind off of it.

It didn't work.

I just could *not* stop thinking about it. She realized quickly this was just one of those times and one of those things that put me in a mood. She canceled the sitter and the date and just let me be. I ended up going on a long walk. When I got back, I was better. It was exactly what I needed.*

No matter how much we all want this to be a simple formula, sometimes it just isn't. That's when we need grace from you, and understandably that's when you need more patience from God. I get that. We get that.

What I'm Not Saying

There's a key phrase in the chart that's important to expound upon. It's the "express how you feel" part. I want to make it abundantly clear that as a family member or friend of someone with anxiety or OCD, you have the right to be heard too. That phrase doesn't just apply to the anxiety sufferer. You also have the right to express your feelings and your frustrations. What's going on is not easy for you. That's OK. My biggest fear in trying to help you navigate all this is that you will

---

* Notice that I invested in myself by getting a little exercise. I didn't just sit around and let the thoughts and frustrations ruminate in silence. I got out. I took action. I did something. I lived out what I suggested you do in chapter 5.

hear that *your* feelings don't matter, that *you* are supposed to "just get over it."

How hypocritical would that be?

In my life, that means Brett needs to be heard when it comes to how my disorders have affected her and the family. The chart can make it seem like the friend or family member bears all the responsibility to "make things right" or to "be careful." That is certainly not the case. The chart is meant to help the friend and family member, not handcuff them. And you, the anxiety sufferer, should not weaponize it against them. If you want your loved one to "be quick to hear, slow to speak, slow to anger" (James 1:19) then you need to be the same. If it is good and healthy for you to be heard, it is good and healthy for your friend or loved one to be heard too. Many times that's the only way to make progress and to live at peace with one another (Rom. 12:18).

Think back to my episode in the coffee shop when I finally realized something was wrong. A big part of that epiphany came when I sat down with Brett and just listened to how my actions were affecting her. It cut me to the core. It was hard and it was emotional. But it was good. I knew I didn't want her to feel that for the rest of her married life she had to walk on eggshells, that she was trapped, and that my feelings and what was going on inside of me were more important than what she was experiencing. Only after hearing her out was I finally able to take the next step toward overcoming my disorders.

Friend, you need to give your loved ones and family members the grace and the space to be heard. As important as it is for them to understand what's going on inside of you, true growth will not happen until you understand what's going on inside of *them*.

That leads me to something really important that I want to say. In fact, Brett told me—very clearly—it needed to be here.

"Tell them they should get counseling," she said. "I remember how lost and alone I felt, and how I didn't know what to say. But once we went to counseling, it's like my whole world changed."

She's right. While I'm glad that you, as someone who is trying to understand their struggling loved one, are reading this book and hope that you find it helpful, I am not a replacement for someone who can dig into what's going on in your life and offer tailored advice. That person for us was our counselor, Mike. Talking with him gave us a common language to communicate with each other. I could better understand what Brett was experiencing, and she could better understand what I was experiencing. Through that, we both found freedom and a sense of rest and peace.

So go to counseling. Go together. Go separately. Go now.

CHAPTER 10

THE FOURTEEN TRUTHS

I'M A LIST PERSON. MAYBE it's part of the OCD. In the content creation business, some of the most-read articles incorporate lists. Not surprisingly, then, when doing research for this project I consistently ran
across "listicles" and found myself gravitating toward the ones that
went something like, "Ten Foods to Avoid if You Have Depression."

Maybe that's part of what my psychiatrist meant in our first meeting when he said, "There's a little OCD in everyone."

Whatever it is, the truth is lists are helpful. They're practical.
They're easy to digest. That's why I wanted to summarize everything
I've learned about anxiety, OCD, depression, and mental health into a
nice, clear, clean, and concise list. This is the heart of everything we've
talked about. However, while some of it is summary, there are also
some new examples and insights within these truths.

Use this list as a reference. Use it to introduce others to the truths in
these pages. Or use it just to remind yourself of what's most important.

1. For Your Good and His Glory

I'm listing this one first because it is the rock that everything else is
built on. It's at the core of this book and at the core of what you need

to understand. It is the only way you will ever make sense of not only your mental health struggles but also any sort of suffering. It's the only way you will ever find any semblance of rest. God *is* working all things for your good and His glory (Rom. 8:28).

We unpacked this idea in chapter 2 (reread it as often as you need to), but there's something else I want to add. To some it may seem obvious, but I have a tendency to overlook or forget it: When you accept and internalize that God is using your struggles for good, you're forced to accept the larger truth that God is *also* good. If He's using your *struggles* for good, you have to accept that *He* is good too. (A bad God can't produce good things.) Why is that important? Because from it flows a host of other truths, like that He loves you and that He is going to take care of you. Once you embrace this, it's easier to see that He's *already* taken care of you. I challenge you to look back for a moment and see how God has been faithful in your life. Maybe it's something He showed you or protected you from. Looking back at your pains may be difficult, but don't let them mask what God has done. It won't be hard to see His hand when you look for it.

I've talked several times about my friend Matt. Well, guess what: He and his family did end up getting the virus. He did not die from it. In fact, his symptoms—unlike those of so many others—were relatively mild. One evening as he was debriefing about the pandemic with his Bible study group and asking how God had shown them evidences of His grace during that time, his wife spoke up. You know what she said?

"I saw God's grace when He allowed Matt to get COVID, because that's when he finally rested, that's when I got my husband back, and that's when our kids got their father back."

It hit Matt hard. It even chokes me up a little.

Sometimes the very thing we fear the most, the very thing we're running from, is exactly what a loving God is using to refine us, to draw us to Himself, and even to restore our relationships. Remember, a *good* God is working for your good and His glory. Embrace that.

2. You Have a Pride Issue

I'm not going to pretend this is easy to hear. Accepting that we may play a part in our struggles never is. (Let me be clear: there's room to take responsibility and own your part while still recognizing some things are going on in your brain that you can't control.)

Baked into the foundation of our anxiety are three types of lies. First, we can figure things out on our own (we don't need God). Second, we're smarter than God (we think what He says to be true isn't *really* true). Third, if we try hard enough, we can make anything work (we're stronger than God). At the heart of all those is this idea that we are superior and don't need His help. That may seem counterintuitive at first, because many of you have come to the end of your rope and are *begging* for help. But until you realize there's pride involved, you're only going part of the way. You're only asking for help up to a point.

Listen, there is freedom in humility. There is freedom in admitting you don't have all the answers, that you can't make sense of it all, that you *must* take God at His word, that your pride is going to tell you in moments of anxiety that the worst thing to do is to wait and take a step back, that maybe help doesn't look exactly like you thought it would (for example, counseling and/or medication). Brokenness doesn't have to be debilitating; sometimes it can be beautiful. But I only experience the beauty of my brokenness when I am exercising humility and admitting where I am deficient and how God is the only one who can fill in those gaps.

3. God Isn't Punishing You

Your anxiety, your OCD, your depression, your whatever else are not punishments for sin in your life. God is not examining your ledger from last weekend and doling out a little anxiety here or a little depression there to make you pay for your bad word, lustful thought, or shameful comment. That's not how this works.

Your mental health struggles aren't sin in and of themselves either. They can lead us into sin, meaning we can act sinfully when we refuse to fight them and instead give in to their lies. So often, though, we convince ourselves that the sin is in the struggle. We feel guilty for even having to battle it. *What kind of person am I? Who thinks like that?* That quickly leads to shame, and shame quickly leads to more fear, depression, and anxiety. Then the cycle starts all over again.

Yes, God has allowed these struggles to happen. But He is faithful to redeem them and redeem you. He is using them for your good and His glory.

4. You Are Broken

For years Brett and I sat under Matt Chandler as members of The Village Church. While he said plenty of things that have stuck with me, I have quoted one thing in particular more times than I can count. It's simple. It's profound. And it oozes truth.

During one of his Sunday sermons, Chandler was talking about how non-Christians like to argue that religion is a crutch for the weak. They so often treat it as a gotcha moment.

But it's the opposite. Here's how he put it:

> One of the things I've heard the world say, and I just want to agree with . . . They're trying to slam us, but it's true.
> *"Christianity is a crutch."*
> I'm like, "Absolutely, because my legs are broken. My legs are busted. I need that crutch."
> *"It's for the weak-minded."*
> "Yes. I have a weak mind. Give me a right mind."
> *"Weak people need it."*
> "Absolutely, weak people need it. Brother, you just don't know you're weak."
> Ultimately, is Christianity a crutch? Yes. Are we crippled? Absolutely.[1]

Friend, your legs are broken. My legs are broken. Our minds are weak. And only God can ultimately heal us, take care of us, and lead us to rest. Stop being concerned about projecting an image of perfection and strength. Remember, we are to boast in our weaknesses (2 Cor. 12:9–10). The sooner we are open about them, the sooner we can begin finding relief. Press into the mess.

5. There Is Hope

A few days after going to my psychiatrist for the first time, I experienced a very heavy moment. It wasn't a depression, but it was more like grief. I began regretting all the "wasted" years I spent spinning my mental wheels. I was grieving over all the time I spent in anxious episodes, in cycles of obsessive thoughts, and I started thinking about what could have been if I had gotten help sooner.

Would my marriage be stronger?

Would I be a better employee? A better Christian?

Would I be a better person?

I also started thinking about the long road ahead and all the work in front of me.

That's when shame started setting in. I started doubting my worth. I felt less than. I started reverting back to the cycle of obsessive thoughts, and they were thoughts about having obsessive thoughts. As I began to sit in those feelings, I remembered something from C. S. Lewis's *The Screwtape Letters*. In one of the letters from the experienced demon, Screwtape, to his underling nephew, Wormwood, Screwtape reminds Wormwood of the power of small attempts to separate the patient (us) from the Creator:

> You will say that these are very small sins; and doubtless, like all young tempters, you are anxious to be able to report spectacular wickedness. But do remember, the only thing that matters is the extent to which you separate the man from the Enemy. It does not matter how small the sins are provided that their cumulative effect is to edge the man away from the Light and out into the Nothing. Murder is no better than cards if cards can do the trick. Indeed the safest road to Hell

is the gradual one—the gentle slope, soft underfoot, without sudden turnings, without milestones, without signposts.[2]

Shame is one of those tiny tools the devil uses to drive a wedge between us and the One who loves us most. When we feel shame, we retreat. When we retreat, we hide. When we hide, we surrender the one thing that can get rid of the shame: intimacy with God.

Inevitably, that shame, that lack of intimacy, makes our battle seem hopeless. But I'm here to tell you that it is not. There is hope even though you may struggle with your mental health for the rest of your life. There is hope because God's promises are true. There is hope because He's offered us tools to fight back. There is hope because there are numerous examples of people like you and me who are learning how to battle against our disorders.

Still, our ultimate hope is not in whether we are healed from anxiety, OCD, or other mental health issues. Our ultimate hope is that God reigns and is redeeming us and our struggles.

Maybe you've heard this before, but it's worth repeating. It's worth burning it into the forefront of your mind and meditating on during those times when your enemy convinces you to give up hope: sometimes we feel like God is digging a grave, but He's really digging a well.

That's why we need to interpret what we don't know by what we do know, and we know He is good.

6. Embrace Tiny Victories

If you're like me (if you're reading this book, you are like me or know someone who is), your anxiety and OCD tell you a lot of lies. One of those lies is that you should be doing more than you're doing or you should have done more than you did. For me that especially plays out in a work context, where I frequently feel like I can be doing more to please my bosses. Once again, that's why people with OCD can be pretty successful in their jobs.

But it also manifests itself in other ways for me, meaning that when I experience a setback I can be especially hard on myself. Here's a reminder that you're going to have setbacks. There are going to be valleys and deserts. And especially in *those* times you need to take your mind off the bigger picture and learn to embrace the tiny victories. When you're climbing out of a crevice, the wisest thing to do is focus on the step immediately in front of you instead of the seemingly insurmountable wall above you.

Tiny victories for me can look like going on a run when I'm anxious or feel myself in the beginning stages of an obsessive episode. It can also mean challenging myself by engaging in a conversation with Brett that has historically given me anxiety, like conversations about money or ways I can be a better husband.

In those moments when I have that difficult conversation, or I do something small to jolt me out of my own thoughts, I celebrate them. Because in the small victories you find the tools to win the bigger battle.

7. Medication Is OK

Many of the heartbreaking messages sent to me after I revealed my diagnosis and my decision to take medication were from Christians who found themselves in a similar spot. Many of them had also been discouraged from taking pills or flat out told they should not. That's why it was so important for me to include the section about my mom's initial response. I've been there. I know what it's like. That's why I want to reiterate this to you now: It is not wrong. It is not an admission of defeat. It is not a sin to take medication for your mental health struggles.

Medication is a common grace, given to us by the giver of all good things. Remember when I said there is hope? Medication may just be the lifeline God is throwing you at this very moment. Will you be on it for the rest of your life? So far I have been. But I'm not consumed with getting off of it. Instead, my focus is on growing closer to Christ. If during that process I no longer have to take medication, then so be it. If not? Then I turn to the words of my favorite hymn: "It is well with my soul."

8. It's an Ongoing Battle

I want to let you in on a struggle I've had in writing this book. It involves a word you may have seen throughout. That word is *overcoming*, or various forms of it. What's the struggle? Well, I've tried to make clear that so far I am not "cured" of my disorder or physically free from my struggle. Instead, I am still on this journey right along with you.

I've tried to be careful to use the future or continuous tense of the word—*overcoming*—but never the past tense—*overcame*. While I believe all these truths can help me overcome anxiety and OCD, I can't say I always follow them perfectly, and I also can't say I have completely overcome my struggles. Remember my story of battling depression when I had to let a former employee go? Guess what: I've had other bouts since then. In fact, one of them came on so strongly and suddenly a few years back that before I knew it, I was on a call with a close friend telling him that I had begun formulating a plan to end it all.

I don't say that to scare you but rather to give you hope. Despite that dark episode, I am still here, I am still battling. I can simultaneously still struggle while also finding some semblance of rest.

It's a paradox. I live—we live—in that paradox. And that's OK. It's the reality of life this side of heaven.

9. It's Never Too Late

A few years back I helped create an online course with Kirk Cameron for parents who are raising children in a digital age. The course featured a man, Mark Gregston, who oversees a ranch for troubled teens. As Kirk asked him about advice he would give to parents who feel they haven't done a good job with their kids, Mark said something that's simple but has stuck with me: "It's never too late."[3]

Friend, that doesn't just apply to parenting. It applies to us. It is never too late to fight back against what's going on inside of you. It's never too late to take care of yourself. It's never too late to throw yourself into the arms of Jesus.

I was twenty-seven before I ever realized what was going on inside of me. I was twenty-seven before I ever started getting help for my struggles. For nearly three decades I had no idea what was going on and no idea how to fix it.

And yet I have learned so much in such a short time. For some of you it's been longer than three decades. That doesn't matter. Pick up your sword and get in the fight.

10. You Need Community

You are not meant to tackle this world or your struggles alone. And yet we fail to grasp that so often. I think that's partly because of the "pull yourself up by your bootstraps" mentality I talked about earlier. It also has to do with the guilt and shame we experience as a result of our disorders. From the beginning of time we have been trained to hide when we feel shame. Just look at Adam and Eve. But our wounds can only be healed when they are exposed to the light, and many times we need others to rip off the Band-Aids.

I mentioned Sinclair Ferguson and his book *Grow in Grace* when talking about community earlier, but he has so many wise things to say on the topic that I want to—or really, I need to—include more. Take a look at these and meditate on them:

- "In order to reflect Christ more perfectly, our relationships with our fellow Christians must be developed!"[4]
- "God's purpose is that we should grow as Christians in the context of Christian fellowship. We need one another in order to show all the facts of what Peter calls the 'multi-coloured' grace of God (1 Peter 4:10)."[5]
- "In Christian fellowship, through the ministry of the word of God, through the care of our fellow-believers, we often discover things about our own hearts which we never anticipated."[6]
- "A closed heart is a major cause of lack of spiritual growth. Only an open heart towards our fellow Christians makes for authentic and natural spiritual development."[7]

One important note: don't let great be the enemy of good. What I mean is that as someone who has served as a church small group leader, I have encountered several people who were group drifters. They would try a group for a little bit, and when it didn't tick every box or meet every expectation perfectly, they would check out and then pull out. They would move on only to eventually repeat the process. Before they knew it, they were in a perpetual search for the "right" group. They would end up blowing in the wind, never anchoring themselves, and many of them suffered because of it, both relationally and spiritually.

Sometimes I think we need to treat community, and especially small groups in the church, like we do marriage. You know who the "one" is for you? The one you have. We have a tendency to over-romanticize "finding our soul mate" and get so caught up in how we feel that we forget the commitment side of the relationship.

During one of our first small groups as a couple, Brett and I were introduced to a young single man named John. He was from India and had come over to the States for a job. He dated a little but never clicked with anyone. One night at our gathering he announced he was engaged. We were shocked. He wasn't dating anyone. I have a tendency to talk before I think, and I'm always looking for a chuckle, so I blurted out, "So did you agree to an arranged marriage, then?"

"Yeah," he said with a straight face. He wasn't joking. His parents and his fiancée's parents—all Christians—had arranged the relationship back in India.

"I just don't have game," John added, explaining why he agreed to it, as Brett shot me the glare that every married man knows all too well.

Today, John and his wife are one of the happiest couples I know. They have two beautiful kids. It all started not because they fell in love but because they chose to love, because they based their love and their relationship on an intentional decision to be a part of each other's lives, to make a covenant with God, and to make it work no matter what.

If they can do it for their marriage, you can do it for your community.

11. Your Struggle Doesn't Affect Just You

Something inevitably happens every time I come through an anxious period, a panic attack, or a depressive episode: I'm reminded how much Brett shares in this struggle with me. If I'm not careful, that can lead to unhealthy guilt and shame. But when I think about it in a healthy way, it's a reminder that these disorders don't affect just me. Other people in my life bear this burden. I need those people, which goes back to the importance of community. But that doesn't always mean it's easy for them.

I said earlier that our anxiety and our depression can be inherently selfish. That wasn't a typo. In every sense of the word, both those things at their worst are overwhelmingly self-focused. They both lead to perpetual navel-gazing.

Remember that. I don't always do a good job of remembering, to be honest. I need to do better. But when you find your community, check in with them about how *they* are doing. Ask them honest questions. Solicit honest feedback about what they're going through, especially from a loved one like a spouse who is battling right beside you. Because their role can often be a lonely one.

I hate to break it to you, but not everyone thinks like you. That means that just as much as you desire grace and patience, you also have to give grace and patience. You'll avoid a lot more frustration if you practice that regularly.

12. Help Others

You know what is one of the most effective exercises for breaking free from a pattern of self-focus and self-pity? Serving others. Did you know that breakthroughs in your disorder can sometimes happen when you intentionally do something uncomfortable for someone you love?

Mike Emlet, the dean of faculty at the Christian Counseling and Educational Foundation, has helped a lot of people—especially Christians—who struggle with anxiety and OCD. He's seen how turning your gaze outward instead of inward can have a dramatic effect. "One of the ways in which growth happens is they [the OCD sufferers] turn outward, and sometimes that's what actually turns the tide in a given moment," he says.[8]

If you feel stuck in an episode, make a conscious effort to sacrifice for someone else. It changes your gaze and your mindset, and can be a gateway to relief. When I was growing up, my stepdad, Mike, would volunteer every weekend at a local nursing home. He would gather all who were willing into a large room, set up a sound system, and sing hymns for them with his guitar. For most of my childhood my sister and I would join him, singing and doing what we could to make the elderly residents feel special. Those are some of the sweetest memories of my youth. Looking back, they occurred during a confusing time when I was struggling with what I didn't know was anxiety. Yet those moments were anything but anxious. From a young age I've seen how serving others brings peace, calm, and joy.

13. God Can Handle Your Anger

As Christians, we do this thing where we forget how ordinary some of the Bible's most prominent figures are. Do you know what ordinary people do? They get angry, and they get angry at God.

Job did. David did. Jonah did. Jacob was so upset, he wrestled an angel all night and demanded a blessing.

We talked about Psalm 13 already, but there are plenty more examples of David getting angry at God. In Psalm 42:9 he asks, "Why have you forgotten me?" In Psalm 142:1–2 he begins with, "With my voice I cry out to the LORD; with my voice I plead for mercy to the LORD. I pour out my complaint before him; I tell my trouble before him."

Remember, you can ask God questions without questioning Him.

That's what laments are, the deep cries of anguish and confusion we talked about in chapter 7. They are the guttural proclamations of our soul trying to make sense of a broken world. God can handle them. He *wants* them, because they bring us closer to Him in an incredibly rich way. There's something beautiful about becoming so desperate that you are willing to pour out all your emotions—the good but especially the bad—to God. Desperation leads to surrender. And only when we completely surrender ourselves to Him can we find rest.

14. Take Care of Yourself

One of my main goals since I've started talking about my struggles has been to remove the stigma of what it looks like to live with mental illness. Recently, there's been good progress made on that front, especially as prominent figures like Pastors Scott Sauls and Tommy Nelson, NFL quarterback Dak Prescott, and tennis star Naomi Osaka (just to name a few) have revealed their own diagnoses and talked about them. That's led to a term and a concept that's gaining popularity, one that I think is especially helpful. It's the concept of taking a "mental health day." You should not be ashamed to take them when needed. Just like your stomach can hurt, your mind can hurt too. It's crucial to be attentive to it.

One of the most important lessons I hope you glean from these pages is that what's going on inside of you at this moment—the fears, the thoughts, the despair—is mental, physical, *and* spiritual. The best way to take care of your mental health is through a regimen that addresses the three facets of it: brain, body, and spirit. That means you need to invest in spiritual remedies as well as physical and psychological ones. Medication can be one of those physical remedies. But there are others: exercise, diet, and rest are just a few. Mental health days are another.

I met a pastor recently whose battle with depression led to a battle with alcohol. It got bad, really bad, and after it was exposed he was put on a reconciliation plan by the elders of the church. Do you know what part of his outpatient treatment plan required? Thirty minutes of exercise every day. If he didn't do it, he failed out of the program.

Your physical health affects your mental health. It's that simple. We've seen that throughout these pages. It is no surprise, then, that I am most at rest when I am physically addressing what I also understand to be spiritual. Do yourself a favor and do the same. Trust me, you'll thank me later.

⌒

Is this the most exhaustive list? Not at all. But I picked these intention-ally because I think they are the "big" ones—they are the truths that seem to lead to a lot of others.

I believe that if you start by embracing these, and are faithful to continually draw closer to the Lord, you are going to start overcoming what's going on inside of you. That will lead to the discovery of other important truths. Honestly, that's the best thing for you. Because when you discover them for yourself, they take root a lot quicker and a lot easier. My prayer is that you will never stop pursuing your mental (and spiritual and physical) health, that God will continually reveal Himself to you, and that through that revelation will come discoveries about Him and yourself that you never imagined.

And when you and I meet—which I hope we do—you can tell me about them too.

THIS ISN'T THE END

WE'VE COME TO THE END of the book. But this is not the end of the story. Especially not my story. And I don't think it's the end of yours either.

There's an inherent danger to concluding a book on a topic like anxiety. The fear is that you treat this as the final word, both for yourself and for me. But if you take these words to heart, this book should only be the beginning.

Many times people who write books or articles on this topic paint an overly optimistic picture of what following their regimen or their program or their set of rules will do for you.

I am not one of those people.

What I mean is that if you meet me at a conference, or if we ever go out to the pub for that drink I mentioned at the beginning, you might say, "Jon, I'm doing everything you talked about. I've embraced the truths, I'm putting into practice what you said, and I'm still struggling." And I would look you directly in the eye and say, "Me too."

This isn't a magic formula. Your journey isn't over. My journey isn't over. I haven't experienced everything I can experience, I haven't reached every conclusion I can conclude, I haven't given you every nugget I will ever think of, and these are not my final thoughts on the topic. While I have begun finding more consistent relief, I am not as restful as I want to be nor as restful as I one day will be. You know how I know that's true? Because up until the day, the hour, the minute that I stopped writing this book, I was still learning, still tweaking ideas, still gleaning new insights and finding places to cram them in. For example, if I had written this book a few years earlier, I would have never been able to talk about depression.

I've used the analogy of these nuggets of truth being like a map, guiding you to the road that ultimately leads you to your destination. How exactly that road winds, what little rest stops it brings you to along the way, I can't say. What I can say is that the principles in this book will at least help your journey make a little more sense and be a little more restful.

As I was thinking of the words to leave you with, I came across a quote from Dane Ortlund that perfectly sums up a key aspect of this journey. It's true that this journey is one filled with self-discovery, but as I mentioned earlier, we can only understand ourselves better when we understand God better.

And that's where Ortlund's words are so important:

> The Christian life, from one angle, is the long journey of let-ting our natural assumption about who God is, over many decades, fall away, being slowly replaced with God's own insistence on who he is. This is hard work. It takes a lot of ser-mons and a lot of suffering to believe that God's deepest heart is "merciful and gracious, slow to anger." The fall in Genesis 3 not only sent us into condemnation and exile. The fall also entrenched in our minds dark thoughts of God, thoughts that are only dug out over multiple exposures to the gospel over many years. Perhaps Satan's greatest victory in your life today is not the sin in which you regularly indulge but the dark thoughts of God's heart that cause you to go there in the first place and keep you cool toward him in the wake of it.[1]

Only when I grasped that idea of discovering God as a lifelong journey did Matthew 11:28–30—the quote from Jesus at the beginning of this book—fully make sense: "Come to me, all who labor and are heavy laden, and I will give you rest. Take my yoke upon you, and learn from me, for I am gentle and lowly in heart, and you will find rest for your souls." I've read those verses many times in my life, but they offered little comfort until now. In the past, they either seemed untrue or were used as a canned response to my struggle. But as I started on this journey to discover what was going on inside me and how to make sense of it, the only thing that helped me do just that was to draw closer to Christ. *That* is when the discoveries happened. *That* is when the truths started revealing themselves. *That* is when I started finding rest.

In other words, as I drew closer to Christ, He became the lens through which everything else became clearer. He shifted my perspective. He changed my assumptions. He reoriented the misguided thinking from my childhood. He gave me a new understanding and appreciation of things like my body, my brain, and common grace.

And as I grow in a deeper relationship with Him, I find myself trusting Him more this year than I did last year. And as I go even deeper, that will not be as much as I will trust Him next year.

In that sense, these words (over sixty thousand of them) will never be an example of how I've arrived. They can't be. The irony of my journey is that while my goal is to change "overcoming" to the past tense and say I "overcame" anxiety and OCD, I may never do that until the other side of glory. Yet if that journey brings me closer to the One who understands me better than anyone else, I have to celebrate that I have not, in fact, arrived. And even admit that maybe that was the goal all along.

That doesn't mean this journey is easy. And it certainly doesn't mean I haven't gone kicking and screaming at times. The process of becoming someone who trusts that God is good is a messy and sometimes ugly one. As Ortlund says, it's a journey that contains some hard stretches, some rocky roads, and some storms that can shake us to our core. There is and will be suffering. It will be difficult. But it will be worth it.

When my son was two, he used to come up to me and raise his little foot as high as he could and say in the sweetest little voice, "Owie. Growing pains." Friend, you will have growing pains. And just like my son could do nothing to stop his, there is nothing you can do to stop yours. You know what the best part about growing pains is? They mean you're growing.

This book, then, has been to help you make sense of those growing pains, to show you how you can mitigate some of that pain, but ultimately to help you rest in what the growing pains mean and what they're doing for you.

If you embrace one truth, let it be this: those pains are for your ultimate good and God's ultimate glory. That's the best news I can give you. It's the best news you can hear. It's the only news that will help you make sense of your disorder and rest, both physically and spiritually, amid the difficulty.

Here's to your ugly, messy, and beautiful journey.

—Jon

ACKNOWLEDGMENTS

WRITING A BOOK TAKES COUNTLESS hours. But I knew that going into it. You know what I didn't realize about writing a book, though? How much those around you have to sacrifice as well. I've already dedicated this book to my wife, Brett, but she deserves another mention here. None of the words you have read here would be possible without her encouragement, sacrifice, and inspiration. Thank you, babe.

I'm also forever grateful to my family, who have allowed me to share my heart as well as the details of some of our darkest moments. Thank you, Mom, Jess, Jeremy, and Josh, for your support. Thank you, Dad, for your words of encouragement along the way. And while most people just put up with their in-laws, I proudly confess that my father-in-law and mother-in-law are two of the greatest people I know. So thank you, Brian and Edie Sanders, for being such awesome cheerleaders, and thank you for letting me use your lake house, where so many of these words were written.

To Keren Baltzer, who was the first person besides my wife who realized I had a story worth telling that others needed to hear. I'll always remember the day you emailed randomly requesting a meeting, and where I was when I picked up the phone and you asked if I had ever thought about writing a book. (For the record, I was pacing outside my daughter's day care.) Thank you for getting this whole thing started.

Many thanks to Cyle Young and his agency for sending out my

proposal to countless publishers and contacts and for continuing to assure me that these words would eventually be printed, and that they would make a difference. You were right.

To my best friend, Tanner Stevenson. You have consistently showed me what it looks like to be a man of God, and you have challenged me to be more than my diagnosis. I treasure our weekly talks (when we both remember) and am even more grateful for our times together. (Except for that one time you helped get me COVID.) Your friendship means more to me than you'll ever know.

Additionally, what you are reading is the work of a team, of which I am just one small part. Thanks to the entire editorial staff at Kregel and their fearless leader, Catherine DeVries, for taking a chance on me. In an era when many publishers are most concerned about social media followers and platform, you let the content dictate your decision-making. I will never forget that.

I will also never forget when I got the first draft back from my editor, Joel Armstrong. Joel, I think I went through all the stages of grief when I saw that document. And while I was reluctant at first to trust you, boy am I glad I did. You made all this so much better.

I'd also like to thank Katherine Chappell and everyone else in the Kregel marketing department, as well as those who served on the titling committee. I'm sure my initial email expressing concerns about the first titling attempt made you wonder if Catherine's trust in this new author was really worth it. I may be biased, but I think it was.

Also, thank you to Billy Hallowell for answering so many of my random calls asking about what to expect during this process, and assuring me that all the back-and-forth, early morning writing sessions, and late-night edits would be worth it. You were right. (Also, make sure you "focus!")

To my friends and sounding boards who have supported me along the way, including James Nordby, David Ubben, Bryan and Vickey Staffel, Trent and Megan Landry, Matt Moore, Arch McIntosh, Steve French, Holly Tate, Dillon Gussis, Daniel Travis, Clayton Maze, Doug Martin, and Joel Voelkert. Thank you.

Special thanks as well to Kirk Cameron for your early support and commitment to getting the word out and for being willing to put your name on the book.

The foundation for this book was actually laid nearly fifteen years ago when my college senior thesis adviser pleaded my case to the administration to let me do something no one had ever done before: use the required project to start writing a book. And while that book isn't the one you are reading today, that experience was invaluable. So to Dr. Ethan Campbell of The King's College in New York City, I will forever be grateful for your vision, your inspiration, and your support. You prepared me well for this day.

I'm not sure how many people have thanked their bosses, but that's exactly what I'm about to do. Two of them in particular have molded me into who I am today, Kathy Leedy and Scott Baker. Without your interest in me not just as an employee but as a human being, I would not be the person I am today. You are both incredible.

And finally to my spiritual family at Providence Church, including the elders who have modeled faithfulness and courage and shepherded me well: Afshin Ziafat, Weyland Glenn, Josiah Foster, Tim Harkins, Mitch Mooney, and Matt Abbink. I'm encouraged and challenged by you daily. Thank you.

FURTHER RESOURCES

Books

Celebration of Discipline: The Path to Spiritual Growth by Richard J. Foster

Fighting Forward: Your Nitty-Gritty Guide to Beating the Lies That Hold You Back by Hannah Brencher

Freedom Starts Today: Overcoming Struggles and Addictions One Day at a Time by John Elmore

Get Out of Your Head: Stopping the Spiral of Toxic Thoughts by Jennie Allen

The Gospel According to Job: An Honest Look at Pain and Doubt from the Life of One Who Lost Everything by Mike Mason

A Grief Observed by C. S. Lewis

Grow in Grace by Sinclair B. Ferguson

I'm Praying for You: 40 Days of Praying the Bible for Someone Who Is Suffering by Nancy Guthrie

Joy in the Sorrow: How a Thriving Church (and Its Pastor) Learned to Suffer Well by Matt Chandler

Morning and Evening: A New Edition of the Classic Devotional Based on The Holy Bible, English Standard Version by Charles H. Spurgeon, edited by Alistair Begg

The Pastoral Handbook of Mental Illness: A Guide for Training and Reference by Steve Bloem

Prayer: Experiencing Awe and Intimacy with God by Timothy Keller

A Praying Life: Connecting with God in a Distracting World by Paul E. Miller

The Problem of Pain by C. S. Lewis

Walking on Water When You Feel Like You're Drowning: Finding Hope in Life's Darkest Moments by Tommy Nelson and Steve Leavitt

When Anxiety Strikes: Help and Hope for Managing Your Storm by Jason Hobbs and Dena Hobbs

Online Resources

"Anxiety: 2019 National Conference USB," Christian Counseling and Educational Foundation, https://www.ccef.org/shop/product/anxiety-2019-national-conference-usb/

Christian Counseling and Educational Foundation, www.ccef.org

Hannah Brencher, www.hannahbrenchercreative.com

"How Does Anxiety Manifest in Those with OCD?" by Mike Emlet, www.ccef.org/video/how-does-anxiety-manifest-in-those-with-ocd/

"OCD with Mike Emlet (Part 1)," *CCEF Podcast*, https://www.ccef.org/podcast/ocd-mike-emlet-part-1/

"OCD with Mike Emlet (Part 2)," *CCEF Podcast*, https://www.ccef.org/podcast/ocd-mike-emlet-part-2/

NOTES

Introduction: Telling the World My Secret

1. Jon Seidl, "It's Time to Tell the World My Secret," *I Am Second* (blog), January 25, 2016, https://blog.iamsecond.com/its-time-to-tell -the-world-my-secret.

Chapter 1: Call It by Its Name

1. Mike Emlet, "How Does Anxiety Manifest in Those with OCD?," Christian Counseling and Educational Foundation, February 28, 2019, video, 5:03, https://www.ccef.org/video/how-does-anxiety -manifest-in-those-with-ocd/.

Chapter 2: The Most Important Book of the Bible

1. Brett Honeycutt, "Reggie White—Minister of Defense," *Sports Spectrum Magazine*, January 26, 2013, https://sportsspectrum.com/sport /football/2013/01/26/reggie-white-minister-of-defense/.
2. *ESV Study Bible* (Wheaton, IL: Crossway, 2008), 1328–29.
3. "Shorter Catechism," Orthodox Presbyterian Church, accessed July 2, 2021, https://www.opc.org/sc.html. Originally written in 1646–47.
4. John Piper, "Our Good Is His Glory," Desiring God, accessed July 2, 2021, https://www.desiringgod.org/articles/our-good-is-his-glory.
5. William Cowper, "God Moves in a Mysterious Way," Hymnary, accessed July 2, 2021, https://hymnary.org/text/god_moves_in_a _mysterious_way. Originally published in 1774.

6. C. S. Lewis, *A Grief Observed* (New York: HarperCollins, 2001), 52.

7. Lewis, *A Grief Observed*, 38.

8. John Piper, "Is Pain Punishment for My Sin?," Desiring God, February 13, 2017, https://www.desiringgod.org/interviews/is-pain-punishment-for-my-sin.

9. Paul E. Miller, *A Praying Life: Connecting with God in a Distracting World* (Colorado Springs: NavPress, 2017), 57.

10. Michael Reeves, "Did You Know That Charles Spurgeon Struggled with Depression?," Crossway, February 24, 2018, https://www.crossway.org/articles/did-you-know-that-charles-spurgeon-struggled-with-depression/.

Chapter 3: The Four Deaths

1. C. S. Lewis, *The Problem of Pain* (New York: HarperOne, 2001), 91.

Chapter 4: The Little White Pill

1. David T. Wong, Kenneth W. Perry, and Frank P. Bymaster, "The Discovery of Fluoxetine Hydrochloride (Prozac)," *Nature* 4 (September 2005): 764, https://www.nature.com/articles/nrd1821.epdf.

2. Jared C. Wilson, "Depression and Common Grace," The Gospel Coalition, August 13, 2014, https://www.thegospelcoalition.org/blogs/jared-c-wilson/depression-and-common-grace/.

3. Sinclair B. Ferguson, *Grow in Grace* (Edinburgh, UK: Banner of Truth, 1989), 129.

Chapter 5: The Physical Battle

1. "8 Ways Running Stimulates Your Brain," Runner's World, June 15, 2018, https://www.runnersworld.com/uk/health/a774414/8-ways-running-stimulates-your-brain/.

2. John J. Ratey, "Can Exercise Help Treat Anxiety?," *Harvard Health Blog*, October 24, 2019, https://www.health.harvard.edu/blog/can-exercise-help-treat-anxiety-2019102418096.

3. "5 Ways the Sun Impacts Your Mental and Physical Health," Tri-City Medical Center, accessed July 2, 2021, https://www.tricitymed

.org/2018/08/5-ways-the-sun-impacts-your-mental-and-physical
-health/.

4. Alice Park, "Why Sunlight Is So Good for You," *Time*, August 7,
   2017, https://time.com/4888327/why-sunlight-is-so-good-for
   -you/.

5. Monique Tello, "Diet and Depression," *Harvard Health Blog*, February 22, 2018, https://www.health.harvard.edu/blog/diet-and
   -depression-2018022213309.

6. Susan Bowling, quoted in Anthea Levi, "Why Drinking Coffee Might
   Be Fueling Your Anxiety," Health.com, December 10, 2018, https://
   www.health.com/condition/anxiety/how-coffee-increases-anxiety.

7. Sarah Schlichter, "9 Foods to Combat Stress and Anxiety," MyFit-
   nessPal, October 16, 2019, https://blog.myfitnesspal.com/9-foods
   -to-help-combat-stress-and-anxiety/.

8. Stephanie Gilbert, "The Importance of Community and Mental
   Health," National Alliance on Mental Illness, November 18, 2019,
   https://nami.org/Blogs/NAMI-Blog/November-2019/The-Impor
   tance-of-Community-and-Mental-Health.

9. Mariska van der Horst and Hilde Coffe, "How Friendship Network
   Characteristics Influence Subject Well-Being," *Social Indicators
   Research* 107 (2012): 509–529, https://link.springer.com/article
   /10.1007/s11205-011-9861-2.

10. Sinclair B. Ferguson, *Grow in Grace* (Edinburgh, UK: Banner of
    Truth, 1989), 76.

11. Amy Morin, "7 Science-Backed Reasons You Should Spend More
    Time Alone," *Forbes*, August 5, 2017, https://www.forbes.com/sites
    /amymorin/2017/08/05/7-science-backed-reasons-you-should-spend
    -more-time-alone/?sh=3ad556721b7e.

12. Nathan Foster, *The Making of an Ordinary Saint: My Journey from
    Frustration to Joy with the Spiritual Disciplines* (Grand Rapids: Baker
    Books, 2014), 67.

13. Ferguson, *Grow in Grace*, 45.

14. David DiSalvo, "Understanding the Connection Between Sleep and
    Anxiety," PsychologyToday.com, December 31, 2018, https://www

.psychologytoday.com/us/blog/neuronarrative/201812/understanding
-the-connection-between-sleep-and-anxiety.

15.   "13 Tips on Getting the Sleep You Need for Good Mental Health,"
      Anxiety.org, October 29, 2016, https://www.anxiety.org/sleep-a
      -fundamental-cure-for-anxiety.

16.   Kayleigh Rogers, "Volunteering Is the Best Kept Secret for Mental
      Health," Vice, December 5, 2017, https://www.vice.com/en/article
      /a37nvk/volunteering-is-the-best-kept-secret-for-mental-health-stress
      week2017.

17.   Rick Nauert, "Too Much Screen Time Linked to Anxiety and
      Depression in Young Children and Teens," Psych Central, Novem-
      ber 11, 2018, https://psychcentral.com/news/2018/11/11/too-much
      -screen-time-linked-to-anxiety-depression-in-young-children-and
      -teens/139931.html.

Chapter 6: The Spiritual Battle

1.   Paul E. Miller, *A Praying Life: Connecting with God in a Distracting
     World* (Colorado Springs: NavPress, 2017), 57.

2.   Miller, *A Praying Life*, 58–59.

3.   Richard Foster, *Celebration of Discipline: The Path to Spiritual
     Growth*, 20th anniversary ed. (New York: HarperCollins, 1998), 17.

4.   Foster, *Celebration of Discipline*, 29.

5.   Miller, *A Praying Life*, 8.

6.   Miller, *A Praying Life*, 8.

7.   Foster, *Celebration of Discipline*, 36.

8.   Foster, *Celebration of Discipline*, 62.

9.   Foster, *Celebration of Discipline*, 63.

10. Sara David, "Counting Every Instance of Rape, Death, and Nudity
     on 'Game of Thrones,'" Vice, September 7, 2017, https://www.vice
     .com/en_us/article/qvvx83/game-of-thrones-by-the-numbers.

11. Anna Holmes, "Skin Is Wearing Thin on HBO's 'Game of Thrones,'"
     Washington Post, April 26, 2012, https://www.washingtonpost.com
     /lifestyle/style/skin-is-wearing-thin-on-hbos-game-of-thrones/2012
     /04/26/gIQA4hd6jT_story.html.

12. Christopher Orr, "Why Does Game of Thrones Feature So Much Sexual Violence?," *Atlantic*, June 17, 2015, https://www.theatlantic .com/entertainment/archive/2015/06/game-of-thrones-sexual -violence/396191/.

13. Jonathan Rothwell, "You Are What You Watch? The Social Effects of TV," *New York Times*, July 25, 2019, https://www.nytimes.com/2019 /07/25/upshot/social-effects-television.html.

14. Jazmine Polk, "How to Deal When Your Favorite TV Shows Trigger Your Anxiety," Health.com, November 15, 2017, https://www.health .com/condition/anxiety/tv-triggers-anxiety-depression.

15. Polk, "When Your Favorite TV Shows."

Chapter 7: A Prescription for the Church

1. Paul E. Miller, *A Praying Life: Connecting with God in a Distracting World* (Colorado Springs: NavPress, 2017), 180.

2. Miller, *A Praying Life*, 148.

3. Miller, *A Praying Life*, 173, 175.

4. Steven J. Cole, "Psalm 13: When God Seems Distant," Bible.org, 1993, https://bible.org/seriespage/psalm-13-when-god-seems-distant.

5. Scott Dickson, "Sunday Morning Worship—July 12," Providence Church, July 12, 2020, video, 1:18:10, https://www.youtube.com /watch?v=wOhFBTqXJoc.

6. Steve Bloem, *The Pastoral Handbook of Mental Illness: A Guide for Training and Reference* (Grand Rapids: Kregel Ministry, 2018), 35.

7. Richard Foster, *Celebration of Discipline: The Path to Spiritual Growth*, 20th anniversary ed. (New York: HarperCollins, 1998), 173.

8. Ben Courson, *Optimisfits: Igniting a Fierce Rebellion Against Hopelessness* (Eugene, OR: Harvest House, 2019), 39.

9. Doris Kearns Goodwin, *Leadership in Turbulent Times* (New York: Simon & Schuster, 2018), 98.

Chapter 9: Help Me Understand

1. Angela Retano, "The Difference Between Fear and Anxiety," Anxiety.org, December 17, 2014, https://www.anxiety.org/fight-or-flight-fear-anxiety.

2. Nassir Ghaemi, "Depression in Command," *Wall Street Journal*, July 30, 2011, https://www.wsj.com/articles/SB10001424053111904800304576474451102761640.

Chapter 10: The Fourteen Truths

1. Matt Chandler, "The Remedy: The Gospel of Jesus Christ," Village Church, August 25, 2013, video, 46:40, https://www.tvcresources.net/resource-library/sermons/the-remedy-the-gospel-of-jesus-christ/.

2. C. S. Lewis, *The Screwtape Letters* (New York: HarperCollins, 2001), 60–61.

3. Mark Gregston, "How to Get It Right," *Engage*, accessed November 24, 2020, https://www.thecouragecourses.com/engage.

4. Sinclair B. Ferguson, *Grow in Grace* (Edinburgh, UK: Banner of Truth, 1989), 68.

5. Ferguson, *Grow in Grace*, 77.

6. Ferguson, *Grow in Grace*, 77.

7. Ferguson, *Grow in Grace*, 79.

8. Mike Emlet, "OCD with Mike Emlet (Part 2)," *CCEF Podcast*, June 13, 2017, podcast, 30:10, https://www.ccef.org/podcast/ocd-mike-emlet-part-2/.

Epilogue: This Isn't the End

1. Dane C. Ortlund, *Gentle and Lowly: The Heart of Christ for Sinners and Sufferers* (Wheaton, IL: Crossway, 2020), 151–52.